PLAYING DIRECTOR

ROY POND

PLAYING DIRECTOR

AN ALBATROSS BOOK

© Roy Pond 1990

Published in Australia and New Zealand by
Albatross Books Pty Ltd
PO Box 320, Sutherland
NSW 2232, Australia
in the United States by
Albatross Books
PO Box 131, Claremont
CA 91711, USA
and in the United Kingdom by
Lion Publishing plc
Peter's Way, Sandy Lane West
Littlemore, Oxford OX4 5HG

First edition 1990

National Library of Australia
Cataloguing-in-Publication data

Pond, Roy
Playing director

ISBN 0 86760 113 2 (Albatross)
ISBN 0 7459 1701 1 (Lion)

I. Title
A 823.3

Cover: Michael Mucci
Printed and bound in Australia by The Book Printer, Victoria

Contents

1

The stranger

DAVE SAT ALONE in the swaying carriage of a steam train, reading a 'pick-your-own-path' adventure story.

The steam engine pulling his carriage went down a gradient, sucking momentum from the line of carriages jostling behind it, tonnes of rolling deadweight constructed of iron and wood and antique brass and filled with tourists out on a day trip. When it hit full speed, the steam locomotive made a scribbling sound as if it were penning its way along the lines like a giant scratchy nib across a jotter.

The writing sound was fitting, Dave thought, with a corner of his fertile mind that wasn't busy choosing the path of the story in his paperback book. In a way he was busy writing as well as reading, turning the pages of the book backwards and forwards as he pursued a story of his own choosing, making choices from those offered to him at the end of each chapter.

'Aren't you a bit old to be reading choose-your-own stories?' a man's voice said at the doorway to the compartment.

Dave didn't know the head-in-the-sand instinct was so strong in him until that moment when, from the blur-tail of his scanning eye, he became aware of a figure standing in the corridor looking into his compartment. He made out the form of a man in his thirties dressed in jeans and a light-coloured safari jacket. He hoped it was a passerby who would move on if he ignored him, but when the stranger stayed at the edge of his vision, Dave began to find it difficult to continue hiding convincingly behind a small paperback book.

The stranger said, 'You can pretend I don't exist if you like, but I'm here and I plan to share the journey with you.' He came into the compartment, put down a canvas grip and dropped onto the seat beside him. Dave lifted his eyes from the page to the stranger's bearded face, trying not to show the disappointment he felt to discover that he no longer had the compartment to himself.

'Hi,' Dave said in a dull voice.

'Aren't you a bit old to be reading pick-your-own-path stories?' the man said again, giving him a close look. Dave, putting down the book, stared unseeing back. His eyes were dreamily focussed inwards as if he were watching a pleasant movie being projected just behind his eyelids. 'They're for little kids,' the man said.

Dave stumbled out of his dream. He flashed resentment at the man. 'You sound like my English teacher. Why am I too old? I like them.'

'What do you like about them?'

Dave, with the ready defensiveness of an enthusiast, was happy to explain.

'In choose-your-own-path stories I play the hero. At the end of each chapter — just at the exciting bits — I get offered two choices, two ways the story can turn. If I want the story to go one way, I turn to a certain page and carry on reading. If I want the story to go another way, I pick up the story at a different page. I can keep reading them over and over again. It's always different. Only I've got to be careful. If I choose the wrong path I can come to a fatal, deadly, final, full stop — a premature The End.'

The stranger winced at his clutter of redundant adjectives and gave a sad shake of his head. 'What's your beef against authors? You not only take over the hero in these stories: you also take over the job of the author. It's literary hijacking.'

Dave revealed the look of dismay of one who has shown another his treasure, only to have it declared dross.

'No, it isn't. It's being in control.'

'You like being in control?'

'Why not? I don't believe in authors. I like choose-your-own-path stories because I get the choices. I get to decide what happens next. I choose my own endings.'

The bearded man, wearing metal-framed aviator style glasses, settled back in the seat, half twisting so that he could look at Dave more easily. He had a faintly amused squint to his eyes. 'Is that what you really want to do — to make all the moves?'

'Course I do.'

'Don't you think you need a little direction in your life? Don't you think everybody does?'

'You really do sound like my teacher. Are you a teacher?'

'I'm a director.'

'Movie director?' Interest sat up in Dave's eyes. 'You mean like Steven Spielberg? I don't suppose. . .' He gasped at the idea. 'You aren't Steven *Spielberg*, are you?'

'No, in spite of the beard and the glasses and the mid-Atlantic accent, sorry to disappoint you. Are you a movie fan, Dave?'

Dave's eyes narrowed in suspicion. 'How'd you know my name?'

'It's written on your bag.'

Dave checked, reminding himself that it was true. The cloth bag he had brought along for his day trip to Victor Harbor was tagged, his name written in the neat, block-letter hand of his sister Janie.

'I love movies. Especially Indiana Jones and James Bond movies. Have you ever seen them?'

'I know them,' the stranger said.

Dave was curious. 'What sort of things do you direct?'

'Oh, people's lives.'

'You mean actual, real, true-to-life, factual documentaries?' Dave said, piling up words again.

'Mostly. I'm big on the truth.'

'What are you doing on the train?'

'A little scouting.'

'For a movie?'

'You could say that.'

'What's the movie about?'

'Depends, Dave.'

'On what?'

'On you.'

'On me? How's that?'

'What do you think it should be about?'

'You're asking me? I have funny tastes. You said so.' Dave waved his paperback book. 'I only read *these*. Can you make a pick-your-own adventure movie where I can choose my own ending?'

'I certainly could.' He fell silent for a moment, then his thoughtful eyes turned excitedly bright behind his glasses. 'In fact, I am making one. It's an interactive adventure about a boy like you whose life suddenly becomes an interactive story.'

Dave looked dubious. 'Who'd watch a movie about a kid like me? Even *I* wouldn't watch it. My life isn't exciting enough. It's not an adventure.'

'But supposing it became one. Imagine your life suddenly became an interactive adventure and you could choose the adventure. Where would your adventure happen?'

'On a train.'

'On a train like this one?'

'No. This is just a Sunday excursion. I'd like a real train journey. On the famous Ghan, travelling to the red heart of Australia and ending up at Ayers Rock.'

Trains don't go all the way to Ayers Rock. They stop at Alice Springs.'

'Then I'd go the rest of the way by road. In a four-wheel drive vehicle.'

'That's just what happens in my movie.'

'Sounds like my kind of story.'

'If it were your kind of story, who else would be in it? Would there be a heroine?'

Dave screwed up his face. 'Maybe. But in adventures they often mess things up by getting into trouble, twisting their ankles and stuff. Although I can't think why. Most girls have pretty strong ankles, especially those who play hockey like my sister Janie.'

'Girls can make things more exciting. You can rescue them.'

'I suppose so. But I'd only want her around if she liked the same kind of stories as I do. And I wouldn't want her to be a pushy type like Janie.'

'Done. What about the heavies? Who should they be? You've got to have conflict in an adventure. How about some aliens who mysteriously appear on board the Ghan to menace the passengers?'

'Aliens on trains?' Dave shook his head with certainty. 'Aliens don't go.'

'Aliens don't go on trains.' He slapped his own forehead. 'Dumb of me.'

'Aliens just don't seem right. If it's an adventure on board a train there have to be enemy secret agents on board. There has to be a scientist involved and secret plans, that sort of thing.'

'Agents. Secret plans. In the middle of Australia?'

'Why not?'

'Okay.'

'It doesn't sound like a documentary.'

'It would be. The hero would have real choices and the movie would go only the way he chose for it to go, moment by moment. It would be live.'

'Actual, real, true-to-life, factual documentary.'

'Absolutely.'

'That'd be great!'

'Maybe I'll put you in it. This could be just the part for an unknown boy like you.'

'Who are you? I don't know your name,' Dave said.

'You can call me Jay. Sorry I don't have a card with me.'

'Where do you live, Jay?'

'All over the place.'

'Are you an Australian film director?'

Yes. And an American one, and a French one.'

'Would you really put me in your film?'

'Could be. I'd like to think about it and maybe get back to you.'

'If you ever need to reach me, I go to Norwood school,' Dave said hopefully.

'I'll remember that. You can go back to reading your book if you want.'

Dave tried to pick up the threads of the story once more, but the stranger had switched points on his train of thought and sent him hurtling along a side track. Dave turned to look at him as if to fix an imprint in his mind. The young man looked past Dave out of the window, watching the blue southern coast slide by.

The carriages swayed as the train made the curved approach to a tunnel, then up ahead Dave heard the hollow, scouring roar as the steam engine entered the tunnel.

The darkness roared around them. Old fashioned electric lamps in the carriage flickered into life then died, leaving them in darkness. One second he was looking at inky particles of blackness that swarmed in front of his eyes, the next he was blinking in bright, calm sunlight that once again filled the compartment. Dave saw that the stranger was gone. He was alone with his paperback book.

2
Hedley

HIS MOTHER DID NOT BELIEVE the story about the director.

'I met a stranger on a train today.'

'Oh yes?' His mother, who was an executive, was busy writing a marketing report on her home computer, her expensive, artificial fingernails beaking the keys like feeding birds. They made a plastic pecking sound.

'He might want me to be in his movie.'

'Really? And what movie is that?'

'An adventure set on the Ghan, travelling to Alice Springs and then on to Ayers Rock by four-wheel drive.'

'You wouldn't happen to be making hints about your birthday next week?'

'It really happened, Mum.'

She stopped working to gaze at him with an anxious look in her clever, dark eyes, eyes that had kind, downturned corners.

'If you're really interested in film directors, why

don't you show any interest in what your father does?'

'Who?'

'Hedley.'

'Him? He only makes ads.'

Dave never referred to 'him' as his father ever since Hedley had left home and even now after he had returned and remarried Dave's mother.

'He's always inviting you to go along to one of his shoots with him, so why don't you?'

'Hedley directs television commercials. He's not a real director. Not like the one I met.'

'I want you to tell the counsellor about this, Dave. You're seeing him again tomorrow. You haven't forgotten about the appointment, have you? It's after school tomorrow.'

'I haven't forgotten.'

His English teacher caught him reading his favourite adventure books during a reading period. It wasn't the first time.

Walking around the class, in between marking papers, Mr Bentley stopped at Dave's desk and looked down the length of his nose at Dave's choice of reading material.

It was clear from Dave's reading habits that he did not believe in *the author*, much less in the kind of author described by his English teacher as having an 'omniscient' point of view, who sat in the sky watching every move and looking into every heart.

'What is this?' Mr Bentley said.

'It's a choose-your-own-path adventure, sir.'

'Not again. Is that all you read, Johnson? Unfortunately, this school does not offer a choose-your-own-path curriculum. Is this the sort of reading likely to get you to university one day?'

There were a few sniggers in the class from those within earshot.

Mr Bentley picked up Dave's book with the long fingers of distaste.

'Choose your own path to adventure, hm?' he read aloud from the cover of the paperback book. 'I suppose this is the logical conclusion of society's drive for equality and independence and its hatred of authority. Now even story characters must be independent of their authors. Well Dave, I do happen to believe in the author, not to mention the author of our lives, and I suggest you rapidly develop an acquaintance with the authors who are required reading for your end-of-term examination.'

'Yes, Mr Bentley.'

In a gentler voice, to Dave alone, Mr Bentley said, 'I'm old-fashioned perhaps, Johnson, but I hope one day you'll learn that it really doesn't matter which way the story goes; what matters is the journey with the author.'

'Yes, sir. Is it all right if I have my book back now?'

Mr Bentley reluctantly dropped the book onto Dave's desk.

Ignoring the magazines spread out on tables around

him, Dave sat in the waiting room of the juvenile counsellor's office absorbed in a pick-your-own-adventure book, one of several that he had brought along with him.

'Hello Dave,' the counsellor said warmly. 'Come into my office.' The counsellor, a tall reedy-looking man, took Dave's record card and file from his receptionist at the reception desk and showed him into his office, sitting him in a big chair. Dave watched him take a chair opposite. 'How old are you now, Dave?' he said, viewing his record card.

'What? Oh, fifteen next week.'

He was still wrapped up in the choose-your-own story he'd been reading. It was running through his head like a river of moving images.

'Aren't you a bit old to be reading such books?'

Not the counsellor too, he thought, coming reluctantly back to the real world.

'Why does everyone grumble about the books I read?'

'Who else grumbles?' the counsellor said.

'Everyone. Especially my English teacher. He says our school doesn't have a choose-your-own curriculum.'

'I can understand his point of view.' He moved on to the purpose of their meeting. 'Tell me, how are things going between you and your father now?'

Dave withdrew, returning to the pleasant movie that was once again screening behind his eyelids.

'I don't have a father.'

'Yes you do. He left you for a while, but he's come

back into your life.'

'My father went away — for good. I don't have a father.'

'Dave, choosing your own adventures is one thing. But we're not free to choose our own fathers. You've got yours and you have to accept him.'

'He's not around. I have no father.'

'Then let me tell you about him. Your father is a commercial film director. He was separated from your mother when you were quite small and he went to America to make commercials. Your mother was married again briefly, but now he has come back to you and your mother. Isn't it exciting having a father who is a film director?'

'I'd like Steven Spielberg for a father.'

'Your father might be another Steven Spielberg for all you know! Don't underestimate Hedley Johnson just because he directs television commercials. A man called Ridley Scott directed TV commercials and went on to direct movies like *Aliens* and *Blade Runner*. Give your father a chance.'

'I don't need anybody. I can make my own decisions.'

'Tell me about your father.'

'I told you he's not around. I don't have a father any more.'

'Then tell me about the one who went away.'

The movie that was screening behind Dave's eyes broke down, but his eyes did not go dark. Instead, a soft glow of memory came into them. 'He was the best. We used to go on train journeys together. We loved trains. We used to go on steam train trips to Victor Harbor. We used to buy fish and chips and eat them on board the horse-drawn carriage on the way to Granite Island. I went on the train myself last weekend. I met a stranger on the train, a real-life film director. He would like me to play a part in his new film. He said so. It's a film about a journey on the Ghan to the red centre of Australia.'

'Ayers Rock. You still dream about Ayers Rock.'

'All the time. But this wasn't a dream about the director. It was a real film director. He's going to see me again when he makes his film.'

'Would you like to have a holiday at the Red Centre?'

'More than anything.'

'Perhaps we should talk to your mum and dad about it.'

'You can talk to my mother if you like, but she's far too busy at work to take time off for my school holidays.'

'I think I'd like to see you and your father together next time. But one thing before we finish. Do you mind if I hang onto one of those books of yours?'

'This one?' Dave looked reluctant. 'I haven't finished it yet. I've only read it three times. It has twenty-seven different endings.'

'I'll give it back to you when I see you and your father together.'

Dave thought a lot about the mysterious director he had met on the train. Would he ever see him again?

He felt sure that he would.

A week went by before he saw the counsellor again. He went with Hedley.

'Do you think I should speak freely in front of him?' Hedley looked a little anxiously from Dave to the counsellor.

'Of course. I think he should know how you're feeling.'

'I don't exist. If he could do it, he'd walk right through me,' Dave's father complained. 'I feel kind of transparent when he looks at me.'

'Yes, I remember the first time I met you and your wife and Dave as a family,' the counsellor recalled. 'Dave climbed into a chair on which you were about to sit. You almost squashed him.'

'It happens all the time. He refuses to see me or listen to me! He'll only listen to his mother. Everything has to be relayed through her. It's weird. At first I thought it was just a game, a snub, but I've tried to catch him out and if he's acting he ought to be in movies because he's a really good actor.' Hedley frowned. 'I'll give you a "for instance". It happened the other night. Dave was about to touch a hot dish in the kitchen. I called out a warning: "Dave, that's red hot and you're going to burn yourself!" He didn't — or couldn't — hear me, and to prove it he went right ahead and burnt himself. Sometimes I pinch myself to see if I'm really here.'

'I don't think he's acting,' the counsellor said. 'I think he's suffering a kind of selective autism where you're concerned. He goes into an inner world of fantasy that shuts you out. It is a totally self-centred world that does not allow for a father.'

'What do I do?'

The counsellor took a paperback book out of a folder and gave it to Hedley. 'Read this.'

Hedley shook his head.

'Don't tell me you're hooked on these adventure books, too.'

'It's Dave's. He let me borrow it. It's an interactive story. Do you know what they are?'

Hedley nodded. 'I've heard about interactive stories. It's a trend. I saw an interactive play in New York. They stopped the play at a vital part and asked the audience to vote by a show of hands which way they wanted the plot to go. Each night the play changes with each different audience. The actors have to rehearse a dozen different endings. There have also been some movies with alternative endings that allow the audience to make a choice.'

'It's not a trend to your son. It's Dave's way of creating a world that is cast a little nearer to his own heart, a world where he is in control. Revealingly, he doesn't believe in "an author". What does that tell you?'

'He's smart. Writers can be a pain. Especially the ones who write television commercials!'

'You are the author he is denying. The author of his life.'

'I'm not an author. I'm a director.'

'Then look at it in director's terms. You represent the direction he is denying in his life.'

Hedley Johnson examined the book, spinning through a few pages. 'You want me to read his books so we'll have something in common.'

The counsellor shook his head. 'I want you to read it so you can enter his world. Try to understand him. Have you ever thought of having a holiday together, just the two of you? Perhaps on a journey together you may find each other.'

'What exactly have you got in mind?'

'Perhaps there are some things we shouldn't discuss in front of Dave. After all, he does have a birthday coming up.' The counsellor turned to Dave. 'You don't mind it if I lend your father your book, do you?'

Dave shrugged. His mind was somewhere else.

'How do you feel about spending some time with your father?'

'Who?'

'Hedley.'

Dave shrugged.

'Then tell me more about this mysterious movie director you met recently,' the counsellor said.

'Are you sure you met a movie director, Dave?' Hedley said.

'He was a real movie director,' Dave said to the counsellor, cornered and sullen.

'Tell me about him, Dave,' the counsellor said coaxingly.

'He's going to make a real movie, like a Steven Spielberg movie. It's going to be about a boy like me and it's going to be the kind of story I like, where I make the choices.'

The two men exchanged throughtful glances.

'Who is he?'

'I don't know.'

'Will you be seeing him again?'

'I don't know. Can I go now?'

'Okay Dave, but think about spending more time with your father. You need to increase the level of empathy, of understanding, between each other. In relationships that's best displayed by a willingness to share in each other's activities.'

3

The film

THAT EVENING, AT THE DINNER TABLE, Hedley mentioned the topic of discussion that had arisen with the counsellor.

'I wonder if Dave would like to come along on a film shoot with me tomorrow?'

Dave let the suggestion hang in the air, like the aroma from their dinner. His mother, who was serving take-away Chinese food into small blue and white bowls, pinned Dave with a stare.

'Would you like to go on a film shoot tomorrow? I think it's important.' Dave shrugged slackly and accepted a bowlful of fried rice and sweet and sour chicken. 'I'll speak to your Year Master and get you the day off school,' his mother suggested.

A day off school? Dave thought. It was almost worth it.

Hedley left the table and came back with a clipboard. Attached to it was a small storyboard with drawn frames indicating scenes from a proposed commercial. He put it on the table in front of Dave who continued eating with his chopsticks. Dave was quite adept with the chopsticks. So was his sister Janie. Having a busy executive for a mother, they were well-accustomed to eating take-away food.

'Take an interest, Dave,' his mother prompted him.

He turned his eyes dully down to the storyboard. It showed sketchy stick drawing scenes of a 'boy-meets-girl' situation and additional scenes of a girl washing and drying her hair.

'It's a commercial for a new shampoo aimed at teenage girls,' Hedley said, explaining the storyline enthusiastically. 'The girl I've cast is a sweetheart. She's an American. An exchange student or something. Anyway, she's at school in Adelaide, an expensive private boarding school.' He pulled out a photograph. It showed a girl with a calm, lovely face and a questioning smile. She had a spill of beautiful dark hair. 'Why don't you come and watch us shoot it? You'd like her, I'm sure.'

'I don't know. I'm a bit behind in my work at school.'

'The term's almost over, Dave. It won't matter now.'

'All the same.'

'Well, I think it's time you made some effort,' his mother said firmly.

The director was waiting for Dave outside the school gates. He sat in a mud-covered four-wheel drive, loaded up with camera equipment, lights and stands and big silver boxes. The vehicle's engine was still running.

The director leaned over and wound down the passenger window. 'Hi. Me again. I've stopped by to put you on notice for a screen test.'

Dave ran happily to the window of the vehicle.

'I wondered if you'd come back. I hoped you would. Are you really going to make a film after all?'

'Count on it,' the bearded young director said, smiling. He was wearing the same blue jeans and pale floppy safari jacket. 'I suggest you brush up your knowledge on Ayers Rock and the area. Do a bit of homework, read a few real books.'

'I don't have any books on Ayers Rock.'

'Then go to your city reference library.'

'And you want to test me?'

'I want to test you.'

'When?'

'Next week. I don't know exactly when, but I'll firm up a time.'

'What do I have to do?'

'I'd rather keep it spontaneous. But I'll tell you one thing — it's a romantic scene with a girl.'

'Romantic?' Dave made a face. 'I don't know about that stuff.'

'Nothing mushy, I promise you. Boy meets girl, that kind of thing. You'll find it all perfectly natural.'

'If you say so,' Dave said dubiously.

'You'll like her. She's a doll.'

'Nobody believes me about you. Do you want to contact my mother or my school? If you chose me for your film, they'd have to know.'

'Your school won't have to know. I'll be shooting it during school holidays. As for your mother — well, tell her by all means.'

A bus tooted behind them.

'I'd better move on; here's your bus. See you later, Dave.'

'But my mother doesn't believe me.'

The director pulled away.

4

The Ghan

DAVE'S TASTE FOR imaginative role-playing even showed in his choice of games.

On the eve of his fifteenth birthday he spent the night playing an interactive adventure game until the early hours of the morning. He would have been late for school had his sister not woken him up. A brisk ten-year-old, wearing glasses, she came into his bedroom to find him still asleep.

Janie's eyes, like bright little fish in bowls, slid around the room, taking in the army of *Dungeons and Dragons* figurines on a table, along with piles of fantasy books and on the wall a familiar big poster of Ayers Rock rising mysteriously out of Australia's Red Centre.

She looked for a moment tenderly at the blond mat of hair of her sleeping brother in the bed.

'Stop dreaming, Dave,' she rapped out. 'It's your birthday. We're waiting at breakfast to see you. Come on, it's an "all family" meeting.'

Dave groaned.

'What time is it?'

'It's 7.05 and if you hadn't played *Dungeons and Dragons* all night you'd be in the shower by now. Do you want to miss the 8.05 bus to school?'

A blue heeler dog jumped onto the bed to lick Dave's nose.

'Hi Ditto,' Dave said, patting the dog. The dog was named 'Ditto' because from the time he was a pup he had always been a great copier with a fondness for duplicating anything Dave did. He now curled up on the bed in the same position as Dave.

'Get off the bed, Ditto,' Janie said sternly. 'You know the house rules.'

The dog ignored her.

'Tell me what I'm getting for my birthday, Janie.'

'Who knows?' she said mysteriously. 'You didn't tell anybody what you wanted, did you? You were supposed to circulate a list of things you wanted so we could choose from it. You didn't follow procedure.'

'Vanish,' he said. Dave aimed a pillow at his departing sister.

'Hurry, the family's waiting for you,' she said through the crack in the door.

Dave patted the dog dreamily.

'I'm a bit tired of this family stuff. You know what I'd put at the top of my birthday wish list, Ditto old mate? If I could, that is. That you and me could take off out of here. . . to the Red Centre.' Dave blinked at the Ayers Rock poster on his wall and gave a sleepy, yet reverent sigh. 'I dreamt about it again.'

Dogs weren't people, but they had people's feelings, it seemed, for the dog gave a small whine that sounded of longing.

At breakfast the family sat in a bright kitchen area. Sunlight spilled into sleepy eyes, coffee cups clinked. It was a modern boardroom sort of table that did not belong in a kitchen, least of all in a traditional colonial kitchen. Dave's mother and father were silently watching him eat. The occasion of Dave's birthday, after the regulation kiss and pat on the back, had drawn as little comment from the family as garbage collection day.

His mother broke the silence as if to explain: 'You didn't make a list, Dave. How did you expect us to know what to give you?'

Janie fixed him with an I-told-you-so look.

'I've already noted our disapproval, Mum,' his little sister said in her efficient, company secretary manner. In a ten-year-old it was poisonous.

Dave's father, Hedley Johnson, cleared his throat. 'Well, Dave?'

Dave gave a disappointed twitch of his shoulders. 'I just thought my family might know,' he said to his mother.

His mother exchanged a smile with Hedley.

'Might know what?'

'I dunno,' Dave said.

'There you are,' his mother said. 'If *you* don't know. . .'

Hedley replied in a playful tone as he scratched his chin. 'Maybe he simply trusts his mother and me to know what's best for him.'

Dave certainly didn't.

'I do, Hedley,' Janie said. She had also fallen into the habit of calling him Hedley. Hedley was her stepfather. They got along well together.

'Course you do, Janie. You're a good kid.'

'Good little company secretary.'

'Don't be rude to your little sister. She might have a nice present for you,' Dave's mother said, opening the door of his disappointment a fraction to let in a little slit of hopeful light.

Was there still something to come, after all?

Dave's mother folded the business section of her morning newspaper.

'I happen to think we know best. We might even surprise you. Maybe it seems I run this home like a corporation, but it's because we both work and we need to have good systems in place. And whatever you may think of me as a mother, I'm a pretty good marketing person — and I never neglect market research. So I think I know what my son wants.'

Dave was unconvinced.

'We've planned a holiday for you, Dave. You're going with your father on the famous Ghan to Alice Springs and then on to Ayers Rock for the school holidays.'

'The Ghan? Brilliant!'

'We're going by Motorail,' Hedley said. 'That means we can take my Land Cruiser on the train with us and drive from Alice Springs to Ayers Rock. It's a long drive — around four or five hundred clicks up the track.'

It only took a bound or two to reach his mother. He hugged his mother, who stiffened inside his boisterous embrace.

'Aren't you going to thank Hedley, too? He wanted to take you. He's taking the time off his shooting schedule to go on the trip with you.'

Hedley took Dave's hand and shook it. 'Happy birthday, Dave,' Hedley said.

Janie said: 'You haven't got *my* present yet. . .

'What's that?'

'Some books to read on the train.'

'Trust my bookish sister,' Dave said.

With an air of great concession, Janie added: 'I've bought you half a dozen choose-your-own stories.'

'Janie, I didn't think you knew!'

'I know. I just don't approve. I think you're too big to be reading them and to be playing *Dungeons and Dragons*.'

Dave hugged his sister.

'You're okay.'

'You're okay, too, Dave,' the little girl said with stern affection. 'But if you think I'm going into the fiery Red Centre with you, you're wrong. I'm going to Grandma's for the holidays.'

Dave remembered something. He sank dejectedly into a chair.

'Oh no.'

'What's the matter, Dave?' his mother said.

'I forgot. There's something else coming up.'

'What?'

'I was waiting to hear from someone.'

'You're not going to bring up that director story again, are you?' she said sternly, a glitter in her eye. 'Come down to earth, Dave. This holiday is real, a chance of a lifetime.' She spoke very firmly, biting off each word for emphasis. 'I am not, repeat not, going to let you spoil it by being silly. You just don't know when to stop, do you?'

She meant what she said. His mother didn't get to be a top executive by knitting and smiling sweetly at people and letting them have their own way.

5

Kelly

THE DAY AT SCHOOL was warm and hazy and Dave's mind filled with images of the red centre of Australia. It would be just like the scene of Ayers Rock that he had on his wall poster at home, he imagined.

After school, he went to the Australiana section of the public reference library in the city. It was a lofty, dim place that smelled of unaired knowledge. It was filled with the kind of books he usually avoided, but this time he wanted facts. He wanted to know all about the magnetic red centre of Australia. A bony, dark-haired librarian sat at a desk like the keeper of this knowledge, daring people to take any from her. Even her golden glasses were tethered on a length of gold chain around her neck.

Dave completed several book request forms and handed them to the librarian who checked them. Golden Eyes sniffed disapprovingly, then shook her head. 'None of these books is available.'

'None of them?' Dave said in disbelief.

The librarian explained in a kind of sick-room whisper that all the books were presently in use. It seemed to give her satisfaction to deny him.

'They're *all* in use?'

'All.'

'I should stick to reading interactive stories.'

'I beg your pardon,' she said, in no way begging or pardoning.

'Can I wait? Whose got them all? How long have they been? Do they need *all* of them?'

'I am required,' Golden Eyes said stiffly, making her glasses flash in an overhead light, 'to answer enquiries about books, but not about the readers in my library.'

'I'm sorry. It's just that I'm leaving for Ayers Rock in the morning and I wanted to read some stuff about the place.'

'Then take a seat and wait,' she said. 'It's up to you.'

Dave prowled the bookshelves, none too discreetly, looking over the shoulders of the various readers who sat with bent heads at the reading tables. He was looking for somebody. He soon discovered the culprit, a girl, with a spill of long dark hair, who sat bent over a large book on Ayers Rock. A pile of other books sat at her slender elbow. Dave stood behind and slightly to one side, directing a current of ill will at her. He began a game of distraction, scraping chairs and coughing behind the girl. He dropped a couple of ballpoint pens and, in the silence, it made the skittering clatter of a ball in a roulette wheel. In between, he pretended to search among the shelves.

He went back to the librarian and enquired again about his book requests in a voice that was far from a whisper. In fact it was modulated to carry to readers on the upper levels of the library, some of whom turned to gaze down at him. He circled the reading brunette to have a look at her and it was then that some of his aggression evaporated. He was surprised to find himself looking at a calm, lovely profile so striking that it made him fumble a book he was holding. It slipped through his fingers, falling to hit the floor with a loud clap that made heads at the reading tables turn and made Golden Eyes add her own silent reproof. Her glasses flashed a signal of warning. But the girl's head remained assiduously bent over her books — *his* books.

There were two choices, two conclusions to draw from her reaction, or lack of it, Dave thought. The girl had remarkable nerves and concentration or else she was playing a game with him. It had to be a game. She must have heard his racket, but she wasn't going to acknowledge it. He wondered if he saw a faint smile visit the corner of her mouth.

The girl was taking notes in a small notepad. He saw her tear off a page and mark a spot in a book. He watched a clock on the wall. The sweep second hand on the clock gave a quiver with each pause, like his own feelings of frustration. He was about to give up and go when finally the girl put back her chair, straightened and walked out. She dropped a sidelong look in his direction as she went. Some girls dropped looks coyly like handkerchiefs, Dave thought, to see if you'd pick it up for them, but there was nothing flirty about the look she gave him. Dave took the full force of frank, amused dark eyes and a questioning smile that stayed with him.

After a suitable interval, he dropped into her empty chair. There remained a quickly fading memory of where she had made contact with the surfaces of table and chair. The girl was real. It was almost a disappointment.

He opened the uppermost book, a large volume with colour plates of Ayers Rock. As he opened it, a scrap of folded notepaper sat up inside the cover.

Dear Restless Boy,
Ayers Rock has been waiting for millions of years,
but I'm sorry to have kept you from it for another
few minutes. Maybe I'll see you there — I'm going
too.

Kelly (Visiting American student)

He slid out from behind the table, scraping his chair back. He ran after the girl. Golden Eyes stepped out from behind her desk as if she were about to stop him with a flying tackle. 'No running in here!' He went through the swing doors and out into the street. There was no sign of the girl. He came thoughtfully back. Golden Eyes shook her head in rebuke. Dave avoided her eye. He returned to the table and sat down. For a while he couldn't settle to reading. The memory of the girl remained, like the little temporary scars of light left on the retina of the eyes when they've seen a match spurt in the dark; Dave tried closing his eyes. The girl's after-image remained there.

The lure of the Red Centre took some time to work on him, but as always the images worked their power and drew him into plans and dreams.

Dave was packing things in his bedroom when his mother knocked and came in.

'I want to say a proper goodbye before you leave in the morning. Your train goes at eleven, don't forget, and Hedley has to take the car to the Motorail ramp at the station two hours beforehand.'

'We know. Don't worry, Mum. Janie's already memoed us with all the details.'

His mother looked around her teenage son's room with the wintry despair all mothers feel about such places. 'I think I'll have this room cleaned while you're away.'

'Please don't — I like everything just as it is.'

She would do it anyway.

'We'll see.' His mother went over to the wall poster of Ayers Rock. 'Your dream's finally coming true, Dave. You're getting there. What exactly do you hope to find?'

Dave carried on packing things into a canvas bag. 'A monolithic rock of great magical and religious significance three hundred and forty eight metres high, nine kilometres around its base.'

'Not that. What do you hope to find for yourself?'

'I dunno. Nothing. Everything. The sacred red

heart of the planet. Some answers to the mystery of life.'

Dave held a pile of choose-your-own books in his hand, the gifts from Janie. He picked out two of them to read first; the rest went into the bag.

'It's not surprising. You've always been attracted to the place. Your father is, too, you know.'

Dave stopped packing.

His mother made a tidy spot where she could sit on Dave's bed. 'There are a few things I haven't told you. A few things I was saving. Ayers Rock is where we met on a holiday. Hedley and I. And it's where he went when we split up. You were too young to remember.'

Dave saw something opening that had long been closed in his life.

'What happened? I've asked you so many times.' He said it in a neutral tone in order to hide his eagerness to know.

'Hedley wanted to make a documentary about Aboriginal legends surrounding Ayers Rock. He took inspiration from the place. Ayers Rock was his Dreaming Place. That thing was like a great big red battery with a power to recharge him. His film-making career was faltering and he wanted to go back there one more time.

'So I told him to go ahead and said that I'd follow him. I was not being honest. I had decided to leave him. I told him not to come back.'

'Why?'

'I was ambitious and devoted to my own career. I

expected him to stay at my side and be supportive. I didn't want to give him the freedom to follow his own career. I was young and a bit selfish, I'm afraid.'

She gave a genuinely regretful sigh. Dave was shocked.

'Didn't he come back?'

'He tried a few times, but I wouldn't have him back. He returned to Ayers Rock to finish the film, then went to America to make television commercials.'

Dave felt an urge to shake those fashionably padded shoulders.

'Don't glare, Dave. It just happened. We never got together again. He wrote to me, but I kept saying no.'

'He wrote and said that I had a heart as hard as that blessed Rock. I often wonder how things might have been.'

'You had it in your hands to change things,' Dave said.

'Yes. I'm sorry, most of all for you, Dave. That's why I wanted you and Hedley to have this holiday. There's a little bit of sentimentality left in your mother's cold heart.'

She seemed to have tired and aged in front of his eyes.

He tried to soften her with a hug; she drew back a little stiffly as always.

'You don't have a cold heart, Mother,' he said, taking pity.

'I do, but maybe we can change the way we are.'

6

Jericho

HEDLEY AND DAVE LEFT EARLY for Adelaide's Keswick passenger terminal, but they did not park with other cars at the Motorail ramp. Hedley had brought a video camera with a microphone.

'I'd like to shoot a bit of background material before they put our car on board.'

Dave looked anxious.

'Don't worry. It doesn't matter if we're last on board. That way we'll be first off at the other end. We won't have to waste a moment of our holiday!'

The Ghan had measured its silvery length along the platform and stretched beyond it to the Motorail section. Hedley strolled towards the train, the camera on his shoulder.

He had explained his reasons for bringing the camera on the drive to the station.

'I've brought a camera and sound equipment along because I want to document our journey together. Don't worry about the camera. Just be yourself. You'll soon forget it's there. I'd like to make a record, maybe a record of our coming together, Dave, so that we can look back on it one day. I want to get it all down on tape and in recorded sound, a sort of video and audio diary. . . all my impressions as I'm experiencing them.'

The Motorail men were loading a vehicle, a white campervan. Two men in checked shirts, obviously owners of the campervan, stood watching.

It was then that Dave heard a soft whine in the back seat.

'Ditto!' He swung around. They had a stowaway. 'You looney mutt,' Dave said, 'you can't come with me on the train!'

Dave instantly saw two choices, two ways things could go. He could report the stowaway dog to Hedley. That would mean taking the dog home and missing the train and perhaps the holiday. Or he could keep Ditto's presence a secret, conceal the dog in the car and let him come on holiday with them.

'Down Ditto,' he whispered to the dog who began to wag his tail. 'Lie low, d'you hear?' He snapped a groundsheet over the dog. 'Not a sound, okay boy?'

Hedley came back, climbed into the Land Cruiser and drove to the ramp. One of the campervan owners in a checked shirt glared at Hedley's four-wheel drive as it approached. Perhaps he also had the idea of being last on board. He had a word to the Motorail attendant loading the van. The attendant promptly backed the campervan off the ramp to make way for Hedley's vehicle.

Hedley drummed his steering wheel in frustration. They were going to load his four-wheel drive ahead of the campervan. He turned on the car radio to ease his frustration.

Dave glanced over his shoulder. Ditto was still hidden under the groundsheet, but the blue heeler was wagging his tail and there was a swaying, rustling bulge under the groundsheet. When Hedley wasn't looking, he wound his window down a fraction to leave air for the dog to breathe, then got out of the car, taking a small bag with the few things he'd need on the trip and leaving his big canvas bag and some camping gear in the car.

It was decided.

Dave was going to the Red Centre and Ditto, the great copier, was living up to his name.

After the shock of discovering the stowaway dog, Dave came upon a pleasant surprise. The blue uniformed steward showed them into a double compartment. Although not big, it was cosy, with a day seat and a fold-down upper bunk, and it had its own connecting shower and toilet. He supposed it was an extravagance his mother could afford.

'Do you want to take a walk around the train?' Hedley said. 'I'd like to shoot some background material.'

'I just want to sit here and watch us go,' Dave said.

'Then I'll see you later.'

It was a grey, drizzly day in Adelaide, not the cheerful send-off he had imagined. He watched travellers and well-wishers go past his window; the well-wishers looked envious, the travellers eager to be aboard.

Some of the glances of well-wishers met his and he enjoyed the envy he saw in them. It was like holding up a mirror to his own excitement, and seeing it deepened the thrill.

When he tired of this, he looked at a brochure that caught his eye on a table. It was a 'Welcome Aboard' brochure giving details about the train and the journey.

He skipped happily through the main points. . .

'The Ghan . . . a legendary train . . . heir to the old Afghan Express and to an even earlier age when Afghans on trains of camels trekked their way into the shimmering Red Centre. The journey, 1559 kilometres in twenty-three hours travelling through some of Australia's most rugged country. . . to Alice Springs and the red centre of Australia. . . the world's last frontier.

It was a call from the heart he had heard all his life and now it was happening. The brochure indicated three stops along the way — at Coonamia, Port Augusta and Tarcoola — and he made a note of these places and the times in between and wrote 'Ditto' next to each stop. He would have to take these opportunities to visit the dog with food and water and, if possible, to let him out for a walk.

At 11.00 am the guardsman's whistle cut through the waiting like a diamond cuts a pane of glass, and the Ghan's big green Australian National diesel drew them out of Adelaide station with barely a warning shudder, swiftly gathering momentum on the seamlessly smooth tracks. Dave watched gracious Adelaide parklands glide past his window. He imagined himself already joined to the Red Centre by the unbroken rails they rode and he imagined Ayers Rock as a mystical, magnetic lode drawing them onwards.

Should he explore the train now or later? He checked his wristwatch. There was only an hour or so to go before lunch and, since the tensions of stowing Ditto undetected aboard the Motorail wagon had left him feeling drained, he decided to relax instead.

He dug out two of the books he had brought for the trip and picked one to begin reading. He could always start the other later. (He enjoyed reading two books at once; it doubled the jeopardy.) Dave settled back to escape. There was something wonderfully abandoning about letting his imagination roam while at the same time escaping bodily aboard the magical speeding train.

The book he had chosen wasn't one of the new ones Janie had bought him. It was one he had read a few times, the one he'd been reading on the steam train when he'd met the director and the one he had lent to the counsellor and to Hedley. It was a spy story set on a train about a secret agent codenamed

Jericho who was being pursued by a vengeful female assassin codenamed Golden Eyes.

He did not see the stranger who came into the compartment and sat opposite him, a dark man with sinister good looks and bleak eyes.

Once he glanced up and noticed that the young man who sat opposite him was holding a gun in his fist. Dave disappeared behind his choose-your-own paperback. The book became unsteady in his hands. The memory of the man and the gun had left a bruise that was tender in the extreme.

The man with the gun spoke. 'I remember reading somewhere that a leopard crouching in a tree only attacks you in that fatal moment when you acknowledge his presence. Ignore him convincingly and he will let you pass. Are you hoping it's the same with secret agents?'

The paperback book jumped in Dave's hand.

'Can't face your own hero?' the man with the gun said.

Now in a bitter voice the stranger began to read aloud from the blurb at the back of the paperback. 'Will you survive this dangerous mission? You are secret agent codenamed Jericho and you are in control. You are on a train with a dangerous enemy agent who has been sent to destroy you. Who will survive this exciting journey? Will you end up being shot in the tunnel by the enemy agent?'

Dave swallowed and said in a tight voice, 'What do you want?'

'I want you to stop acting like an ostrich and come out of hiding.'

That was when Dave made his decision and came out from behind the book. He regretted it at once. Whatever flicker of hope he might have had of the stranger's good intentions flickered out when he found himself looking into brutal, impaling eyes. He had dark, lounging good looks, polished and devil-may-care; he looked like something straight out of a spy adventure — the one Dave was reading.

Dave said, looking at the gun, 'I don't know if that's a real gun, but you shouldn't point it. What do you want? Who are you?'

'No point keeping you guessing. Jericho's the name,' he said.

There was a pause as Dave digested this incredible piece of information.

He decided to humour the stranger. 'Hi Jericho, how're you going? I knew it was you all along.'

'Shove that,' Jericho said. His eyes slitted dangerously. 'Think I'm a nut? Could be you don't have another think coming.'

The stranger lifted the gun fractionally.

'Sorry,' Dave said.

'Careful.'

Dave, his eyes livening in excitement, stared at the stranger. 'What are you going to do?'

'I'll tell you. It's not very original. I'm waiting for a tunnel further down the line. . .'

'Oh, oh. . .' Dave said.

'When we get inside I'm going to. . .'

Just like the book?'

'Exactly.'

Dave slumped into silence. The stranger said in a goading voice, 'Are you going to give up just like that?'

'Why not?' Dave said.

'You're the one who wants to be in control, to make all the twists and turns,' he taunted. 'You want to make all the choices. Which page will you turn to? Want to find some smart way out, don't you? Some last minute inspiration. Is that it? You want to keep me in suspense?'

'Not really.'

But he went right on speculating. 'Wonder what you'll try to do? A desperate savate kick in the nick of time? Perhaps you're carrying a concealed knife?' His eyes darkened suspiciously. 'Or do you just happen to be carrying another choose-your-own book hidden inside your shirt, protecting your heart?'

Dave started to edge towards the compartment door.

The stranger continued. 'I wonder what you'll try? A visit to the washroom where you can signal out of the window with a streaming toilet roll perhaps? Or. . .' He sadistically let Dave move almost five centimetres closer to the door. '. . .try to make a dive for the door, but don't because I've caught you at it,' he said in a tired voice.

Dave smiled awkwardly and watched the eye of the .38 dilate until it looked as big as a tunnel.

The man who called himself Jericho disgustedly

shook his head. 'If that's the best you can do I don't know why you want to be in control.'

'I'm only fifteen,' Dave said. 'I haven't had much experience, you know.'

'Experience? You've got me into dozens of scrapes like this,' he said peevishly. 'You didn't care how I got out of them. What about that time you locked me in the guard's van with twelve karate killers? All very well for you to turn to another page. I had to find my way out. . .'

'Sorry. . . I made a wrong choice there.'

'And while I'm getting things off my chest, did you have to skip over the scene where I was in the compartment with the beautiful lady spy? Isn't anything sacred?'

'I didn't think you'd like her — I don't like mushy bits.'

'That's because you're only fifteen! What about *my* feelings? When I pull this trigger, don't forget the cold-blooded torture and the roughings-up you've put me through,' he reminded Dave unpleasantly.

He was coldly angry. His eyes were glowing like polar lights.

Dave tried to pacify him. 'I never meant to upset you. And don't forget, when I was in control I gave you life and made you walk and breathe. I even gave you speech.'

'You gave me inverted commas!'

'I don't like lots of speech in stories.'

'Well, there's been too much speech in this one, but

it'll end very soon. I'll get even. You let an enemy agent shoot me in the tunnel. It's a betrayal.' His voice shook with disgust.

'Sorry, I didn't mean to end the story so suddenly. It was a mistake. I made the very worst choice and came to a final full stop.' Dave looked guilty. 'It happens sometimes. That's the fun of choose-your-own stories.'

'It may be fun for you.'

'Can't we be friends?' Dave held out his hand. 'I really am sorry.'

The young man waved the gun around the compartment threateningly. 'Keep away from me,' he growled. 'Think I'd trust you for a second? I don't like people who try to take over my role and I've waited for the moment to get even with you. Nothing's going to stop me now.'

The stranger's eyes never left Dave's face. He seemed to be watching and waiting for some sign of something. Fear? There was none of that in evidence. The boy's face was lit up like a funfair. The stranger glanced at his watch.

'Two minutes left,' he said. 'Two minutes before we reach the tunnel and my finger curls around the trigger.'

'That's enough,' Dave said, tiring of the man's threats. 'We're going into the middle of Australia where there are no tunnels, so put that gun away. It's over.' Dave closed the book he was reading with a snap of finality. 'Besides, you should know by now that we're both on the same side.'

7

The opportunity

DAVE ROAMED THE LENGTH of the train, rolling like a ball in a pinball machine down narrow corridors, glancing off the walls with the occasional swaying of the train, only to bump into varied and colourful obstructions along the way, tourists and holidaymakers of several nationalities. Above the beat of the train he heard Japanese, American and European accents in the corridors.

The train was running close to full capacity. There were children and mothers and fathers, elderly holidaymakers and a group who looked like conventioneers. A glance into each compartment — most had their doors open — was like looking at a series of tableaux of happy travellers.

One door was just closing as he looked in. He glimpsed the face of a dark-haired woman with gold-framed glasses that were held around her neck on a length of gold chain. From the glare she threw him, it was evident that she remembered him, too. The door slid firmly shut.

Golden Eyes. What a coincidence that the woman from the public reference library was also on the train.

He stopped roaming when he reached the Ghan's entertainment car where he stopped to look around with interest. There were a few adults feeding poker machines, some kids playing Scrabble and Trivial Pursuit at one of the tables in the games room and an elderly woman sitting under a hair drier in the small hairdressing salon. There was also a souvenir shop and video hire shop and, next to it, a partitioned lounge with TV sets and comfortable chairs where passengers could sit and view their choice of movies, listening to the sound on headphones.

Dave squeezed into the tiny souvenir shop next to the salon, joining some passengers who were looking at the books, magazines, souvenirs and videos for hire. He ran an eye over the range of videos. Among the new releases, on a rack out of reach behind a counter, he noticed an old favourite, *Indiana Jones and The Last Crusade*. It would be fun seeing it again in such novel surroundings.

'Can I take a look at *The Last Crusade*?' he said to the assistant.

'*The Last Crusade* — yes, I'd like that, too.'

Two voices spoke at the same time; his own, and another that belonged to a girl with a spill of dark hair who turned a well-remembered smile on him.

'You.'

'Hello, restless boy.'

'I got your letter.'

'Now what letter was that?' she said playfully.

'The one you left in the book. I went outside to find you, but you were gone.'

'I was in a telephone booth watching you.'

They both laughed.

The girl at the counter held out a videocassette for their inspection.

'Go on,' the girl said. 'I made you wait once. You see it first.'

He wasn't going to let the girl get away twice.

'No, you.'

'You can look at it together — on the same monitor,' the shop girl explained patiently, with a knowing smile. 'You can hire two sets of head-phones.'

'After lunch?'

'Why not?' As if on cue, the lunch announcement for the first sitting cut through on an intercom.

'Kelly,' she said, sticking out her hand a little mannishly. 'See you after lunch. I'm on the second sitting for lunch. You?'

'First.'

The girl left with a departing smile that would console him all through lunch.

'My name's Dave,' he said to her departing back. 'Dave Johnson. . .'

The video shop assistant agreed to reserve the video for a 2.30 screening and she also agreed to a second request. 'Do you have any spare plastic bags?' he asked of the video shop assistant.

The girl scratched under the counter. She

produced some plastic bags. 'Will these do?'

'Perfect. Thanks.' They would make useful doggy bags for Ditto.

Dave went back to the compartment. It was empty. He went on alone to the dining car, taking a seat near a window. The cereal fields of South Australia slid flatly past. He took out a plastic bag from a pocket and opened it in his lap. The dining car steward brought some bread rolls to his table. He chewed on one while two others went swiftly and secretly into the bag on his lap.

'Expecting to develop an appetite between now and dinner?' a voice said. A man slid into a seat opposite Dave. He was a young man with a beard and aviator style glasses and he wore jeans and a light coloured safari jacket.

'I knew you were going to show up again. I just knew it.'

'I'm glad I didn't disappoint you. You're expecting a famine, I see. I've never seen bread rolls disappear so fast.'

'I'm starving.' The waiter took their orders.

'What are you doing on the train?' Dave said.

'I'm on a journey — just like you. A journey inwards.'

'Are you still making that film?'

'Could be.'

'When?'

'It could be happening right now on this train.'

'Right now, here, this very second, this moment?' Dave said, having his usual pile-up of words in his enthusiasm. He swung around, looking for places where the fixed round eye of a camera lens could be hiding. 'Where are your cameras?'

'Haven't you heard of hidden cameras?'

'Like the show *Candid Camera*? I don't believe it.'

'Suit yourself.' The young director unfolded a napkin and spread it on his lap. 'Why are you eating alone? Where's the man you came on board with? Is that your father?'

'Hedley? No. He went for a walk. Maybe he went to the bar for a drink, I don't know. I don't care. He can eat at the second sitting if he wants.'

'Taken a walk around the train yet?' the young man asked.

'Yes.'

'Meet anyone interesting?'

'As a matter of fact I did. I bumped into a girl, a girl I met yesterday at a library in Adelaide.'

'Did you say library? One of those places where they keep real books? Books that have a beginning, a middle and an end? Your reading habits must have taken a turn for the better. Did this girl happen to be quite striking with long dark hair?'

'How do you know about her?'

'I noticed her. She's cute.'

Their food came.

'Is that a cereal crop growing out there?' Dave pointed distractingly out of the window, slipping a portion of roast beef and gravy into the bag.

The director followed his line of vision. 'I expect so.'

'Look at that farmhouse.'

'Hm.'

'Is that a scarecrow?'

'Okay, that's enough. I've got a question for you. Is that a doggy bag you've got under the table? Don't tell me you've smuggled a dog into your compartment?

He looked at the director with respect. 'You get onto things fast, don't you?'

'I notice things. A good director has to have an eye for detail. There's a saying about architecture that's also true of films and books — God is in the details.'

'Okay, I'll let you into my secret,' Dave said with the relief of one confessing, 'if you keep it to yourself.'

'Go ahead,' the man said.

'I *have* smuggled a dog on board. Only not onto the train itself. In the Motorail section. He's in our Land Cruiser. I didn't mean to bring him. He's a stowaway.'

'Then I must call the steward,' the bearded man waved. Dave tensed as the steward came over. 'This roast beef is terrific,' the director said. 'Any chance of having another serving if I promise to skip dessert?' He winked across at Dave.

'No worries, sir,' the steward said. 'And you needn't skip your dessert.'

'Good, I'm nuts about chocolate mousse.' When the steward left to fetch a second serving of roast beef, the director said, 'My contribution to your doggy bag.'

'Thanks,' Dave said, 'you're a friend.' The two shared a conspiratorial smile.

'We can't let Ditto starve, can we? Yes, I know his name. I know a lot about you, Dave. I find out things. I feel I know you. In fact, I feel I know what you're thinking even before you think it. You've shared a secret; now it's time to share one with you. You like adventures, Dave; you like to make all the choices, don't you?'

'I told you.'

'Then here's your chance to pick your own plot. You still like the idea of a spy story? Well then, what kind of story should it be?' Dave became aware that the Ghan had slowed. It stopped with a wave-like shiver of its silver muscles and gave a faint hiss. 'Take your time. As you can see, the train has stopped. In fact, look around and you'll see that more than the train has stopped.'

It was true. People had stopped, too.

The passengers in the dining car, even the stewards had stopped; everybody around them was frozen in arrested gestures. They seemed to be waiting for something, like actors waiting for a cue from their director.

Was this man controlling them? Dave felt a nudge of fear under his ribs.

8

Golden Eyes

'WHO ARE YOU?' DAVE DEMANDED, leaning forward in eagerness where another boy, a more sensible one, might have shrunk in horror.

'The director, Jay. I told you. Will you join me in a game?'

'I'll join you all right. Games don't frighten me.' Some of his nerve returned, although now tinged with awe. 'And yes, I still like the idea of a spy story.'

The director appeared to think about it for a moment. 'Then here's the scenario. The girl you met is an American student. She's been attending a private boarding school in Adelaide. Her father is a key electronics scientist involved in the sensitive US installation at Pine Gap, involved in Star Wars and other top secret projects. She's going to Alice Springs on this train and then travelling by bus to meet her father at the Yulara resort near Ayers Rock where they are going to spend a holiday together in the Northern Territory.'

'A scientist? Good. There must always be a scientist — or at least a set of secret scientific documents.'

'Her father thought a train trip to Alice Springs and then a bus trip to Ayers Rock would be fun for her. But she has been targeted by enemy agents. They are after the scientist's daughter. They will almost certainly try to nab her, maybe take her off the train, and use her to make her father hand over top secret Star Wars documents.'

'You mean they'll steal her, carry her off, abduct and kidnap her and hold her as ransom?' Dave said, throwing a traffic snarl of words together.

'All of that.'

'I like it. Whose agents are they?'

The director spread his hands. 'Who knows? Middle Eastern? IRA? Be on your guard. Kelly is in real danger. Your codename is Jericho and it's your job to protect her.'

'What happens next?'

'You'll get your choices, Dave.'

The train moved on again. 'I'm going to look for Kelly,' Dave said, sliding out from behind the table.

'Are you going to skip dessert?'

'Yes.'

'But it's chocolate mousse.'

'I'm too excited.'

'Oh well, you won't mind if I have yours.'

He passed Kelly in a corridor as he was leaving the dining car and the second sitting filed in for lunch.

'Enjoy your lunch,' he said. 'I'll see you later.'

'What's for dessert?'

'Chocolate mousse.'

'Brilliant. I'm nuts about chocolate mousse.'

He turned and took a half step forward when he bumped into a dark-haired woman coming down the corridor towards the dining car.

'You stupid boy. Look where you're going!' The woman's gold-framed glasses flashed angrily.

'Sorry.'

She gave a sniff and followed Kelly into the dining car. It was Golden Eyes from the public reference library. Was she the enemy agent who was after Kelly? Was it possible? Who would suspect a librarian? He stopped in the corridor.

The director followed him out. 'It's choice time, Dave. First choice: stay outside the dining car and keep a guard on Kelly. Second choice: slip off the train at Coonamia and take Ditto his lunch. It's a ten minute stop. There should be time. He's going to get hungry — and thirsty — sitting in the car.'

'But I need to do both — guard Kelly *and* look after Ditto.'

'That's what choices are all about.'

Dave looked for some clue in the bearded face of the director, but there was none, only a light of bright curiosity behind the aviator style glasses.

'See you around, Dave.' The director moved on.

At around 2.00 pm the train stopped at Coonamia. Dave was nailed to the spot by indecision. It was his mission to stay and guard Kelly. Yet it was his duty to take care of poor Ditto.

Ditto. Before he made another move, it was time to attend to Ditto. Dave jumped off the train as soon as it had stopped, doggy bag in hand.

With only a ten minute stop scheduled at Coonamia, Dave hurried down the length of the platform to the double-decker Motorail wagon, blinking in the bright afternoon sun of a sky that had cleared. He loitered on the platform, picking a moment when nobody at the station was looking before he swung himself aboard the car transporter.

Ditto must have known he was coming. The blue heeler was standing up at the window, steaming up the glass, even though Dave had left the window open a little for air. Dave gave the dog, who squealed with delight, his freedom. 'Sorry, old boy. I'll bet you've been going cross-eyed waiting to take a walk.'

Ditto nuzzled the plastic bag with his nose. 'Yeah, I've got some dinner and water for you, too, but first a walk.'

Dave and the dog slid past the white campervan at the end of the wagon. He leaned out to check the line was clear on both sides then, satisfied it was safe, he jumped down and Ditto followed. Ditto lost no time expressing his relief and gratitude on the dust-coated iron of a wheel. 'Good boy. C'mon, old mate, back in the Land Cruiser. We don't want to be left stranded in Coonamia.'

He dug among the camping gear in the back of the four-wheel drive and produced a couple of dishes. In one he served the roast beef from lunch.

The other he filled with water. With a final pat he locked the door and slipped back onto the platform. The whistle shrilled before he reached the passenger section.

He jumped on board and threaded his way down the corridor to the dining car. Lunch was still in progress. He stood in a corridor looking out of a window. Guests started to file past. He waited. No Kelly. No Golden Eyes. He went into the dining car to look around.

'Second sitting's finished,' a steward said. 'Sorry. You'll have to wait till dinner.'

'Did you see a girl in here?'

'Lots of girls.'

'This one was about my age, pretty, with long dark hair. She was alone.'

'The steward, a large, jolly-faced man with a mottled skin like a pork sausage, shook his head. 'No girl on her own. But I did see a girl with her mother. I noticed her because her mother demanded a glass of water for her daughter when the girl took a turn.'

Dave went uneasily to the entertainment car to wait. He remembered the last time he waited for the girl in the public library. Perhaps she was a girl who always made you wait.

It was strange about Golden Eyes being on the train as well. He had seen Kelly and Golden Eyes go into the dining car together, but neither had come out, at least not while he was there. Perhaps neither of them had found anything to tempt them on the menu and had left early. No, that wasn't right, he thought. Kelly was 'nuts about chocolate mousse'.

He remembered the steward's reply to his question. There had been no girl on her own, only a girl with her mother. A girl with her mother. That was it. People might come into the dining car alone, but they couldn't stay alone for long. Others soon joined them. Had Golden Eyes sat next to Kelly? Had the steward therefore assumed that she was the girl's mother? Or, more ominously, had Golden Eyes misled the steward by claiming to be her mother? Perhaps Kelly was the girl who had taken a turn. Perhaps Golden Eyes had slipped something into the girl's drink.

Dave left the entertainment car and rattled off the sides of the corridors in his rush to Golden Eyes' compartment, almost bowling over passengers on the way. He stopped outside her compartment. It was at the end of a carriage and he had no trouble finding it.

The door was closed. He knocked and waited. The door looked boredly back. He recklessly opened it, just a bit at first, feeling a kind of raw-edged excitement. At the slightest pressure from his hand the door opened and, like a vacuum, the darkness within ripped him inside, hands taking him down to the floor. A sack with ropes at the mouth was thrown over his head and tied around his arms tightly. He was pushed onto a seat and his legs were also secured.

He heard a muffled cry. Kelly. She sounded scared. There was a scuffle and drumming sound of somebody kicking against a seat. Then the door closed and he heard departing footsteps. Dave wriggled in the bag. He was alone in the compartment.

He was still struggling to free himself when the train made its next stop at Port Augusta. Had they taken Kelly off the train? He renewed his struggle inside the confining black hold of the bag. The Ghan gave a blast on its horn and snaked out of Port Augusta, leaving Dave with a sense of hopelessness. Fortunately there were holes in the bag allowing him to breathe.

Hands undid the bag.

The sound of the speeding train returned and with it, after the stuffiness of the bag, fresh air and light.

'Jericho.'

'You're not very good at this, are you?'

'I'm glad you've stopped being silly. You've decided we're both on the same side after all.'

'It's just a truce until this job is over. Then you and I have some unfinished business.' Dave found himself looking into the dark, wily face of the secret agent code-named Jericho.

'You didn't have to undo me. I would've wriggled out,' Dave said, complaining.

'Sure.'

'They've taken the girl. Golden Eyes is behind it.'

'Golden Eyes?'

'That's a code-name.'

'I know that, but how do you?'

'I saw her go into the dining car with Kelly.'

'You've actually seen Golden Eyes? We've fought

each other for years, but I've never set eyes on her. Describe her to me.'

Dave obliged.

'That'll do. I'll search the train and look for her. I'll go into every compartment. I've borrowed an Australian National Steward's uniform so I'll be free to snoop around. Meanwhile, keep out of trouble. I haven't got time to rescue kids.'

It was six hours before the next stop at Tarcoola. Dinner time came and passed. He did not eat, although he did walk through the dining car looking for Kelly. Dave began to feel a slight cloying of his excitement. He was losing his grip on the game, he thought. It was the way he felt when he had been reading the same adventure too long, turning the pages this way and that, half forgetting where he had come from and growing careless about where he was headed. He was losing his instinctive edge and that's when accidents happened. That's when you turned the wrong page and came to that fatal deadly final Full Stop. But this was no time for The End. He had to find Kelly. She had sounded scared and he was growing scared for her.

Dave walked the length of the train at first quickly, then dallyingly, lingering in corridors outside partly open doors. He passed Hedley in a corridor.

'Where have you been, Dave?'

'Walking.'

'We're supposed to spend some time together. How about joining me to watch a video?'

'No thanks. I like walking around.'

'Really?'

'Really.'

Hedley shook his head and walked on. 'See you back in the compartment.'

'Excuse me,' a steward said in a corridor, passing him.

'Jericho!'

Jericho winced. 'Not so loud.'

'Any sign of Kelly?'

'None. I've checked every compartment. Either she's been whisked off the train or they're playing musical compartments very cleverly — no sign of Golden Eyes either. But I'll keep looking.'

Dave went forlornly back to the entertainment car where he found the director watching a video, listening to the sound on headphones. Glimpsing the boy from the corner of his eyes, he tore off the headphones and said with genuine concern, 'How does it go, Dave? Still hanging in there?'

'No sign of her.'

'They've got her tucked away all right. I wonder where?'

'Don't you know?'

'You're making the moves. You're directing things.'

Dave flopped into a vacant chair beside the young man. 'I think it's time to call in the conductor and tell him what's happened.'

'The conductor?' The director clucked in disappointment. 'You want to hand over to somebody else already? Calling in the conductor at this point would be like calling in the publisher to stop a book, or a producer to stop the film. *You're* in control, Dave. You want to make the choices. How are you going to handle it? Did you see anything of your attackers?'

'I saw nothing but the inside of an old bag, that's all,'

'What kind of bag?'

'A tent bag.'

'Well, that's probably a clue.'

'You think so? I'll bet the train is full of campers.'

'Don't give up yet.'

'Is this truly what you say it is,' Dave said edgily, 'or is Kelly just hiding somewhere to tease me? Am I caught up in something?'

'Of course you're caught up in something.'

'I mean a real story.'

'Of course it's a real story. Stories don't fake it. They're governed by laws of internal logic as rigid as the laws of nature herself. All stories are real stories. That's not to say all stories are real. . .' he shrugged. 'You'll have to make up your mind about this one.'

'You're making my head spin.'

'Look out there, Dave. See those distant lights? That's Woomera, an old rocket base where man once stood on tiptoes to reach for the stars. It's a fitting seat of exploration, out here in Australia's heart, in a landscape that's as close to outer space as you'll find on this planet. There's a resounding presence in all that emptiness. It was not for nothing that the prophets and wise men of old took themselves into the wilderness of Israel, a wilderness not unlike this. The greater the emptiness, the greater the space for content.'

Dave gave a shiver. Looking out at the specks, mere dustings of light in the endless dark, filled him with a giddy emptiness. 'I'm scared, Jay.'

'Yes.'

'I'm going to go on looking for Kelly,' he said. 'I just hope she's still on the train.'

Morning of Day One

This is a record on tape of a journey made by a father and a son, of two people who belong together yet, like the parallel lines of a railway, never meet at any point, converging only on some illusory horizon. But where is that horizon and when do we ever reach it? Perhaps the convergence I hope for is only wishful thinking. Dave and I seem hardly to touch.

He looked excited when we packed the car and drove to the station today; it started out hopefully enough. He was so excited he almost forgot to kiss Margaret and Janie goodbye.

He didn't even say goodbye to Ditto, his dog. There was no sign of Ditto when we left this morning. He usually operates like a Xerox machine with Dave. Whatever Dave does, Ditto does likewise. Yet Dave didn't even miss him.

I was disappointed Dave didn't want to get out of the Land Cruiser when we reached the terminal. He seemed to be holding back. Was he having second thoughts about going?

Then once on board, he turned down an invitation to explore the train with me. Instead, he curled up with one of his fantasy books. Will this journey help me to break through to him?

I hardly saw Dave this morning. I met an interesting colleague at a bar on the train just before lunch. He's a producer on the lookout for a new project and we quite lost track of time as we threw around some ideas. I think we could end up working together. He was interested in this 'living documentary' I'm shooting — the story of the journey that Dave and I are making and the reconciliation we're hoping for.

Saw Dave a few times wandering abstractedly down corridors. I can tell he's wrestling with events. Perhaps he's finding the idea of reconciliation difficult and he's feeling trapped. I suggested he join me in watching a video, but he had that look in his eyes, the look he has when his mind is busy following twists and turns in a story of his own choosing.

I didn't press the matter. I must give him as much freedom as he wants.

9

Ditto

THE GHAN STOPPED at Tarcoola just before ten o'clock that night. It was a thirty minute stop.

Dave remembered Ditto.

He was suddenly regretful that he had skipped dinner, not for his own sake, but for that of the blue heeler. Now he had no food to give him. Well, at least he could give him another drink. Hopefully, without exercise, the dog hadn't worked up an appetite.

He left the train at the platform, hoping for a glimpse of the girl. Few passengers joined him to stretch their legs. Most were in bed, sleeping through till their arrival at Alice Springs in the morning.

Dave walked down the platform along the length of the train, passing the silver carriages. The sides were emblazoned with the symbol of an Afghan rider on a camel. It was the Ghan's logo, a tribute to the camel trains of the past. Light still glowed behind a few of the shuttered compartment windows. The majority lay in restful darkness. He turned several times to look for Kelly.

He came to the Motorail wagons, skeletal garages on wheels with cars and trucks and vans stacked in tiers. The temperature had dropped. Dave rubbed his arms. He passed the last car at the end of the wagon, the white campervan, and turned to walk back. The windows of the campervan were steamed up. So were the Land Cruiser's, he noticed. It was no doubt the change in temperature after the heat of the day. Nights could be achingly cold in the centre of Australia.

Ditto had heard him coming. He gave a yelp of pleasure. Dave climbed onto the wagon, went past the white campervan and opened the Land Cruiser door. The dog jumped up, its paws on his shoulders, licking his cheeks. 'Sorry to keep you waiting, Ditto boy. Want another walk?' He took the dog to the end of the platform where he found a patch of bare earth. 'Not long now, Ditto. After this, it's just a bit of shut-eye and we'll be arriving in Alice Springs. Then we'll see who gets off this train.'

Dave gave a noisy yawn. Ditto copied him.

Hedley approached him in a corridor after the train pulled out of Tarcoola.

'That's enough wandering around for one night, young Dave. Bed for you.'

'Okay,' Dave said.

'I kept the top bunk for you.'

'Thanks.'

Dave climbed into the top bunk and switched on a small reading light. Although he actually felt too tired to read, he wanted to enjoy the experience of reading one of his favourite stories in bed on a train. He also hoped to shake himself free of his worries about Kelly.

He began a new adventure, one of the stories Janie had given him. He reached the end of the first chapter where two choices were printed at the bottom of the page. If he wanted the story to go one way, he had to turn to a certain page. If he wanted it to go another way, he had to turn to a different page.

Which way to turn, he wondered, blinking at the page. He felt a flare of resentment, the first time he had felt it in reading one of his books. At that moment, after all that had happened, he wished he didn't have to choose, that the story would pull straight ahead like the locomotive pulling their carriages, running strong and true instead of twisting and turning and constantly throwing him onto side tracks. The two choices printed at the bottom of the page swam in front of his eyes. Too hard. He was just too tired. He'd make a mistake and regret it.

'Switch off your light now, Dave, and get some sleep. We pull into Alice Springs pretty early.'

There was no answer.

Normally, to sleep on that legendary train, of all trains, scouring through the Australian night, would have been like passing through a tunnel of gently buffeting dreams, but not on that night. Dave felt as if he were passing into and through the entrails of a silvery serpent that periodically convulsed and squeezed the breath out of him. They were all in his dream — Kelly, the director, Ditto, even the steamed-up cars on the Motorail wagon — all trapped inside the serpent's gut, like Jonah in the whale, a story his grandmother had once read him from the Bible. But he could never quite reach Kelly who was always separated from him by a twist in the lining of the serpent like the links in the skin of a sausage. He could see Kelly through the skin, but only hazily, as if the skin were steamed up by her breathing.

End of Day One

Dave skipped supper. Couldn't eat, he said. Finally I had to drag him into the compartment.

'What's on your mind, Dave?' I said. I wondered if he'd share things with me.

He wouldn't answer.

He went to sleep in the top bunk reading a pick-your-own-path adventure. He fell asleep with the book on his chest and I had to climb up and turn his light off.

In the night, he gave loud yells. One was so shrill I sat up in the dark and banged my head on the bunk above my head.

Is this trip a nightmare for him? I hope not. It wasn't supposed to be that.

He's obviously finding things more difficult than I thought.

Awakened by his cries, I lay thinking in my bunk, feeling the rhythmic shake of the carriage. It jogged memories, reminding me of the times I used to take him on steam train rides to Victor Harbor, before the split-up.

It also reminded me of the steam train ride we'd taken a few weeks ago. It was the counsellor's idea. He suggested Margaret and I take Dave on a nostalgic steam train ride to Victor Harbor to give Dave's memories and emotions a stir.

It had been years since I'd been on the steam train ride to Victor Harbor and if it left Dave untouched, it certainly got to me. I was moved by the reliving of a memory. But Dave continued to ignore me. It was as if he sat alone in the antique train compartment. We bought fish and chips at a shop in Victor Harbor and ate them on the horse-drawn tram that trundled along the windswept causeway to Granite Island.

On the way back to the railway station, Margaret saw an ice cream shop and gave Dave some money. 'Buy us each an ice cream cone,' she said to the boy, partly because we were all hot, but also as a test. He went into the ice cream shop. Margaret and I waited outside. She didn't mention her hidden motive , but I had guessed.

'I can hardly stand the tension,' I said.

'Neither can I. I can't imagine what he'll choose for me,' she said innocently, not letting on to her hidden motive. 'I hope I get one with a chocolate flake in mine.'

Dave came out with two piled ice cream cones, one for himself and one for his mother.

'Sorry,' Margaret said to me, disappointed.

'See what I've got to put up with? I'm just not here.'

'Never mind. If it's any consolation, I didn't get my chocolate flake.'

The ice cream Dave had chosen for her was dipped in hundreds and thousands as if it had been rolled in multi-coloured sand.

We boarded the train for the return trip to Adelaide. The day trip had shown no evidence of reaching Dave. He had brought along one of his books and he buried his nose in it, spinning the pages backwards and forwards as he followed his path to adventure. I knew I would have to try something more dramatic. That revealing episode was a mere week ago.

And now here we are on Dave's dream train, the Ghan, and it's drawing us into the heart of Australia. I wonder if it'll draw us any closer together?

Dave awakened early, showered, changed and went to breakfast in the dining car. Hedley joined him.

'Are you feeling all right, Dave?'

'Fine.'

'You look a little grim. I heard you cry out in the night. Aren't you enjoying the train trip?'

'I'm enjoying it.'

'I really wanted us to enjoy this time together, Dave. We have such a lot of space to fill between us. I thought, hoped, that maybe this train trip could put us back on the right tracks.'

'It's a magical train,' Dave said. 'I love it.'

'I'm glad, Dave. Now cheer up.' As they were leaving the dining car after breakfast, The Ghan aimed itself between the gunsight vee of Heavitree Gap and finally reached its mark, its targeted destination of Alice Springs. Dave and Hedley took their bags off the train. Dave dragged his feet. He kept looking at passengers leaving the train, trying to catch sight of Kelly.

'Come on, Dave, we've got to get the car.'

'Coming.' He stopped to tie the shoelaces of his sneakers with elaborate and protracted care.

Nobody else was leaving the train. The passengers had all spilled out of the carriages. Where was Kelly? Had they spirited her away at one of the stops? Dave felt a sour tang of despair in his stomach. This was not the ending he had wanted. He'd wanted to save Kelly. Had he made the wrong turning somewhere? Where was the director? And what choices could he possibly offer? 'I've failed, struck a disastrous The End right at the beginning of the story,' he thought.

'Is that case too heavy for you?'

'No, I can manage.'

'Don't want to leave the train, do you? Never mind, we still have the return journey to enjoy.'

The Motorail men drove the cars off the wagon onto a ramp and parked them nearby. Hedley and Dave stood watching. 'Funny,' Hedley said, filming their Land Cruiser as it came off the train. 'Our car windows are steamed up. Odd. The windows of an empty building, or an empty car, don't usually steam up.' He left Dave's side. 'Think I'll get some shots of the cars coming off from another angle,' he said over his shoulder.

Dave went to their Land Cruiser. Ditto stood up, wagging his tail. 'Not yet, boy, you've got to stay down just a bit longer.' He covered Ditto with the groundsheet again, hoping to conceal his presence until they were clear of the station. Ditto gave a soft whine of disappointment 'Sh. . . sh. . . A few more moments, that's all. Lie down.'

There had been no sign of the girl. They must have taken her off the train at one of the stops. Where was Hedley? He rubbed the steamed-up windscreen of the Land Cruiser, a steamed-up window that had almost given away the dog's presence. Smart of Hedley to have noticed, he thought. He was pretty sharp.

Then the force of what Hedley had said hit him like the delayed crack at the end of a long whip. Empty cars didn't steam up. Then why had the empty white campervan been steamed up last night? He checked the campervan, offloaded first and parked ahead of their car. Its windows were steamed up! Now things made sense. Dave and Jericho had been unable to find Kelly on the train because *she wasn't on it*. The kidnappers had hidden her in the Motorail section. They'd shut her in the campervan. It explained the tent bag when the two check-shirted campers had attacked him in the compartment.

The director came around the other side of the car. 'How does it go?'

'Kelly's in the campervan. I've discovered her kidnappers.'

'Good work. Then it seems you have two choices. First choice: call Hedley and try to convince him to give chase. Second choice: take off after them right now.'

'But I can't drive.'

'Jericho can. He's standing back there, watching you. Call him.'

Dave followed his line of direction and saw Jericho on the platform pretending to read a tourist map. Torn, Dave looked back at the campervan. Two men in checked shirts were climbing into it.

'But I just can't leave Hedley here.'

'He left you once, didn't he?' The engine of the white campervan kicked into life. 'Make it snappy, Dave. Choose. Is it the girl or Hedley?'

'I can't make a choice like that. . .'

'You must.'

The campervan pulled away from the station.

'I don't know what to do.'

'Even no decision is still a decision. Everything stops.'

'Where are they going in the campervan?'

'I can't say.'

'I know. They're taking her to Ayers Rock to trade her for the scientist's secrets.'

'Could be.'

'Won't you tell me?'

'It doesn't happen in choose-your-own stories.'

'There's only one road to Ayers Rock. We'll catch

up with them.'

'It's possible, I suppose. See you later, Dave.' The director went.

Hedley climbed into the Land Cruiser and blinked at the sight of Ditto sitting up with his paws over the back of Dave's seat.

'Ditto? You smuggled Ditto on board! You little sneak, Dave! Is that why you kept disappearing?'

'I didn't smuggle him on board. He smuggled himself on board. When I got into the car, he must have slipped in, too. You know how he copies me. I found him in the car at Adelaide station.'

'Why didn't you tell me?'

'I thought you'd cancel our trip. I didn't want anything to stop it.'

'Well, he's here now, so I guess I'll have to accept it. Hello boy,' Hedley said, rubbing the blue heeler's head. 'You really are a copycat dog, aren't you?'

They set off for Ayers Rock.

10

The road train

'CAN'T WE GO A BIT FASTER?' Dave said, peering anxiously ahead. The road stretched out like the silvery slime-thread of a slug's trail shining in sunlight.

'You're in a hurry to get there.'

'Do we have to go so slowly?'

'We're riding on the speed limit as it is. Sit back and relax. It's a long, long drive.'

They passed cars, caravans, trucks, even campervans, but not the white one.

The road reeled them slowly inwards towards Ayers Rock, through the vibrating emptiness of Australia's heart.

Dave wondered if he should tell Hedley about the girl and the white campervan and also about what had happened on the train. Would that be breaking the rules? Hedley would take over, tell him what to do. He would no longer be choosing his own endings — that's if he was still choosing them anyway. Things were passing out of his control.

Hedley grew more mellow and relaxed as the hours went by.

'This part of the world has always excited me,' he told Dave. 'It's always had a power for me like a giant red battery.'

They passed some kangaroos, leaping in effortless arcs as if suspended on wires as they went across the plain.

'Do you know how the kangaroo came to have such long back legs? The Aboriginal people tell a story about it. Kangaroos didn't always have long back legs, they say. It was an accident, a freak event. Once, many thousands of years ago, before the Dreamtime, a great storm with violent winds swept over the Australian mainland. It tore up trees and threw clouds of dust and grass many miles high into the air. A herd of kangaroos fed in the open when the storm hit. It sucked them up into the sky like so many leaves, transporting them far over Australia. The kangaroos struggled to get back to the ground, stretching their back legs lower and lower in their attempts to touch the earth, but as soon as they touched down, another blast would take them up again in a series of hooping leaps. They tried and tried as they journeyed through the heavens. The more they struggled to land, stretching and stretching, the longer their back legs grew. When the storm finally died, they came down to earth looking the way they do today.'

'That's a made-up legend, just a tale, a false myth and a fable,' Dave said, word-stacking again, 'and it's just not true.'

'The Aboriginals believe it. I reckon I do, too.'

They approached the speeding turmoil of a monster road train. Hedley slowed and fell in behind it for a few kilometres. They were tricky things to pass. This one was half the length of a city block, a chain of roaring, articulated steel slabs rolling on sets of tyres as wide as logs. A few approaching cars forced Hedley to remain patiently behind it.

He waited for his chance to overtake. A checked sleeve of a man's arm appeared out of the window of the road train's cab, signalling the all clear and inviting him to pass.

Dave stiffened, grabbed his seat. He stared at the back of the truck. Hedley pulled out and began to move past. Dave's eyes locked onto the truck. Hedley was halfway along the silvery length of the road train when he saw another truck suddenly grow in his windscreen, rolling towards him like a boulder. It was too late to drop back, but if he kept going they would ride into steely oblivion. Hedley tugged on the steering wheel, veering off the road and into the scrubby red bush, slewing around in a half-circle before stopping.

'The idiot!' Hedley banged the steering wheel. 'Why did he signal me to overtake if there was a truck coming? He must have seen it.'

Dave was not surprised. He'd expected nothing less. Hedley switched off the engine. He climbed out. Dave followed numbly and Ditto followed his lead. The road train and the truck were now speeding away in opposite directions, stretching an invisible cord of tension that twanged with the nearness of a disaster.

Hedley checked the Land Cruiser's tyres to make sure they hadn't ripped on the stony surface.

The hot Land Cruiser ticked as it cooled, making tiny cracks in the silence. Ditto made his signature wetly on a back wheel.

'Ditto, you've got the whole of Australia around us and you have to go and do it on the wheel!' This time, Dave copied Ditto — not on a wheel, but behind a scrubby bush.

'Let's catch that road train,' Hedley said. 'I want to get its number. That driver's a car killer.'

They jumped back into the Land Cruiser and drove back onto the road. Hedley went quickly through the gears and settled back to cruise at the legal speed. The road train must have increased its speed, putting some distance between them. They did not see it again until a few hours outside Uluru. It sat parked like a beached whale at a roadside garage and diner.

Hedley stopped the Land Cruiser not far from the parked monster, scribbling the number on the back of a card.

'Stay here, Dave.'

Hedley got out of the car, walked around to the cab of the road train. He came back, shrugging.

'I'll take a look in the diner. Would you like me to get you a drink?'

'Thanks,' Dave said.

Dave opened his door tentatively. Kelly was in the monster, he was sure of it. How else could he explain the disappearance of the white campervan? The road train had swallowed it up and taken it on board to confuse anyone following. He climbed down onto the baked apron of cracked earth that surrounded the station.

'Stay, Ditto,' he said.

Too late. Ditto emulated his action and slipped out beside him. Dave circled the road train from the opposite side. The cab was empty. On the other side he bent to look under the belly of the beast, examining the ranks of rubber tyres lined up under its crushing weight. He saw a pair of legs on the other side walk along the length of the road train. Ditto growled. Dave bent, restraining Ditto by the collar, circling to keep out of view. He saw a corrugated iron shed marked 'Toilets'. The man had come from a washroom.

Dave went around the back of the shed and peered around the corner of the road train. Ditto also poked his nose around it. A man in a checked shirt was opening the trailer at the back of the road train. The man took a quick look inside, then, apparently satisfied, began to close the heavy steel doors. He never had a chance to slide the heavy bolt home. Ditto, sensing Dave's fear of the man, broke free from his grasp and ran at him, snapping at his heels. He took hold of a trouser leg. The man danced. He broke free. A well-aimed kick took some of the fight out of Ditto, who yelped and retreated, still growling.

The man went into the diner.

The director came out of the toilet shed and around the corner, wiping wet hands on his jeans. 'I suppose you can't expect to find a hand drier out here in the land of nowhere.'

'Jay!'

'How does it go, Dave?'

'I don't know what to do. It's going wrong.'

'You want choices? Okay. Choice one: climb aboard the back of the road train so you can try to find a way to rescue Kelly from the inside — if she's in there.'

'I'm sure she is. But what if they drive away before I can get her out? Where will they take me? Hedley won't know where I've gone.'

'He may figure it out. He's pretty suspicious about the road train by now.'

'Choice two?'

'Immobilise the road train and buy time.'

'How do I immobilise a road train?'

'Run around and let the air out of its tyres.'

'There are hundreds and thousands and millions of tyres on that thing.'

'A slight exaggeration.'

'I might only have time to let down one tyre before they come out. They'd hardly notice it.'

'That's a chance.'

'I don't know, Jay.' He licked his lips.

'You'd better make a decision,' the director said in a playful sing-song way. 'Time is ticking by.'

With a quick sideways check on the diner, Dave

made his decision. He ran towards the road train. Ditto, naturally, copied him.

Neither of them saw Jericho going around to check the cab of the road train.

11

The campervan

DAVE OPENED THE HEAVY DOORS with an effort. Ditto leaped straight inside. Dave hoisted himself up, using a bumper as a foothold, and climbed into the warm gloom of the interior. He ground his teeth in bitterness. He expected to discover the white campervan inside. All he could see was a load towards the back, bulking under canvas covers. Footsteps approached from the diner. There was no time to close the door. Somebody saved him the trouble. It went dark inside as it closed with the ringing bang of a prison gate and he heard giant bolts grate home.

Should he bang on the doors and own up to his indiscretion before it was too late?

The beast rumbled into life. Maybe somebody could still hear him. He set up a hammering with both fists on the metal walls of the truck's insides. Ditto added to the din with shrill barks that bounced around the metal walls.

The truck shuddered under his feet as it left the

diner and climbed back onto the road.

He was locked in the blackness of an empty truck in the land of nowhere — and that's exactly where he was going, nowhere.

Where was the director when he needed him? Which way did he turn now? Not knowing which way to turn had a whole new meaning for Dave.

Day Two
Perhaps the journey on The Ghan touched some nerve in Dave after all. I tried to make him share things with me.

He was reluctant to leave the train and he kept turning to look behind him as if he couldn't drag his eyes and himself away from it. Then when we set off for Alice Springs, he sat on the edge of his seat, peering ahead up the slowly unwinding road.

'What are you looking for, Dave?'

'Nothing,' he said.

'Well, there's plenty of that out here. Look all around.'

When we saw some kangaroos, I tried to close the gap between us by telling him some of the Aboriginal legends I had heard when I was making my documentary about legends of the Red Centre. He listened, but only with half a mind.

We caught up with a massive road train, a hurtling monster so big that when we drew into its shadow, its boiling slipstream seemed to suck us closer. 'I won't overtake until it's safe,' I said, slowing to sit behind it. Then the driver's arm came out and gave us a wave to go past. Dave stiffened and gripped the edge of his seat.

'Relax, Dave.'

We moved out beside the road train. Dave's anxiety didn't recede. His eyes were boring into the back of it. I put on speed to overtake it. Dave raked the side of the road train with his stare as we went by.

That was when the truck came out of nowhere barrelling towards us. I swung off the road and into the scrub.

Dave took it all as a matter of course as if he'd expected nothing less. We followed the road train and caught up with it at a petrol station and diner. I parked some way behind it, then went around it. There was nobody in the cab. I went into the diner and bought some soft drinks and snacks for the rest of our trip.

A man in a checked shirt, coming into the diner, pushed past me at the flyscreen door.

I went back to the Land Cruiser. Dave — and Ditto — had gone. I sat there sipping my drink, giving them a bit of time.

The dog was a comfort. Dave squatted with his back against the vibrating steel wall, hugging Ditto who echoed his mood of despair with sympathetic whines.

It was like the time when he found himself tied up in the tent bag. Everything looked black. There was not a gleam of light in the truck.

'I've been a thick-head, Ditto. That tent bag obviously belonged to campers. That was a clue that was supposed to have led me to the campervan, but I missed it.' He slapped his own leg. 'Dumb, dumb, dumb.'

Ditto licked him. The darkness was thick and heavy and airless and it had a texture like a curtain pressing against his face. He felt that he could almost scratch it with his fingernails. There was no darkness like darkness of your own making. He had plunged himself into this. It was like the darkness and secret 'aloneness' he had always held inside him.

There was no way to turn and nobody to turn to. I'm in total control of my own disaster, he thought bitterly. There was no guiding hand to help, only himself. He did not even have anyone to blame. Being free to choose was what he'd wanted. He wanted to decide the twists and turns, to choose his own endings. He'd chosen this.

Over the miles, he imagined he was sliding deeper and deeper into the darkness and that the darkness he was sliding into was a darkness inside himself. Was this The End, to sink and be lost without trace in the darkness of yourself? He squeezed the dog for comfort. Ditto gave a cry. He became aware of a tapping, like the sound of a blind person approaching behind a stick. It hadn't just started. The sound had been there when they'd sat down. At first he'd explained it away as a noise made by a rattling bolt, but there was a pattern to it. There it was again: *dum tiddy dum dum — dum dum*. Perhaps road trains like railway trains made their own internal music, rhythms set up by metal sinews on the move. He would have expected a loose bolt to rattle, but this sound was precise. The beats were organised and carefully picked out. *Dum tiddy dum dum — dum dum.* It was an oddly human rhythm for a loose bolt to make. He turned his head on one side to listen. Ditto yelped excitedly.

There was somebody inside the truck.

Dave drew himself cautiously up. The tapping sound came from the back of the hold. He went forward. He stumbled into the cargo that bulked under covers. He squatted and lifted one corner of a cover. Reaching inside, his exploring hand touched the nubbly tread of a vehicle wheel. There was a car under the tarpaulin. Was it the white campervan? Was Kelly inside, signalling to him? He gave a tap on the outside. The tapping was answered like a far-off echo. He tapped again and the response came back quicker. He tapped a third time and the answer was immediate.

He eagerly tugged aside the covers and groped for the door. His fingers met a vertical edge and travelled past it until they met a handle. He gave it a twist. It opened. There was a muffled sound from within. Dave climbed into a seat. It was the driver's seat. He bumped against a steering wheel. He needed to find a light. The van must have one. He ran hands like blind crabs over the inside of the cab. His fingers met a bulbous shape in the ceiling. With one finger he searched and found a tiny wheel that turned with a click, snapping light into his eyes.

Kelly lay on a mattress with tape over her mouth and she was secured hand and foot.

12

The chase

DAVE FELT PLEASED with himself.

'Sorry I've taken so long. I've been on your trail ever since you left the dining car. Where's Golden Eyes?

'Golden Eyes?'

'The woman with the gold glasses on a gold chain around her neck.'

'She's the one who drugged me in the dining car! She put a needle in my arm and I went to sleep at the table. I never saw her again. When I came around I was tied up and gagged. Then at the station I was carried to the Motorail section and put into this campervan.'

'I knew it.'

'How did you know? And whose dog is that? I heard him barking.'

'That's Ditto, my dog. A professional stowaway. He was also riding in the Motorail section, just like you.' Dave explained how the dog had sneaked on board the Land Cruiser.

Kelly gave Ditto a pat. 'You poor thing. I know what you've been through.'

Dave looked around the campervan. The vehicle was as well appointed as a luxury caravan with its own kitchen and sleeping area and even a portable toilet.

'You've been in here all that time?'

'Yes, with a few spells to stretch my legs.'

Kelly's face, previously calm-looking, was now not so much calm as dazed and immobile.

'You look groggy.'

'You lose touch with all feelings left alone in the dark,' she said.

'I'm going to get you out of here,' he promised.

'How?'

'At the next stop. When they open the doors I'm going to start up the campervan, put the gears in reverse and shoot us out of here like a missile — with us inside it.'

'You're under age. You're not allowed to drive.'

'Who's going to stop me? I can't drive in a public place — but the inside of a truck isn't a public place. Once we've crashed out, we'll drive off the road, stop in the bush and go on foot from there. They can't follow us in a road train. They'll be on foot, just like us. We'll outrun them.'

'I hope I can run. I'm awfully stiff.' She rubbed the bottom of her legs. 'I feel like a statue.'

'You're not going to go and twist an ankle, are you? You're not supposed to do that. I made a special point of it.'

She was puzzled by his words. 'What do you mean?'

'Nothing. I just mean you'd better stretch your legs so you'll be ready to run.'

'Thankyou for coming after me. And saving me. It was very brave of you.'

'I haven't saved you yet. But I'm going to do my best. Do you known why they kidnapped you? Is it because of your father?'

'How do you know about my father?'

'He's a scientist, isn't he?'

'Yes, but who told you?'

'I must have heard somebody mention it,' he said evasively. 'Perhaps one of the check-shirts who attacked me in Golden Eyes' compartment.'

'They attacked you?' She touched his arm concernedly. 'I hope they didn't hurt you.'

'No, they couldn't touch me. They tied me up, but I got free.'

'You're very clever! I tried and tried, but I couldn't do it.'

'You can do anything if you know which way to turn,' Dave said. 'What exactly do they plan to do with you?'

'I heard them talking. They're planning to meet my father at a deserted farmhouse called "God's Peace", half an hour away from Yulara, and make the hand-over. An exchange of my freedom for my father's secrets. '

'What time are they meeting?'

'At dusk.'

'We've got to stop your father from handing over the secrets. I hope they'll stop this road train soon and open up the back doors so we can try to make our escape.'

The road train streamed like a blast of silver metal through the heat of the day.

'Sorry we didn't get to see the video together,' Kelly said. 'You must have thought the worst about me.'

'Yeah, I did. I thought you were starting to make a habit of keeping me waiting for things, like the time in the library.'

She managed a wan smile at the memory. She seemed to be brightening. In spite of her hours of confinement in the bottled heat of the van, her dark hair still shone cleanly in the overhead light.

'If we get out of this, shall we go to Ayers Rock together? We can join my father. Who are you travelling with?'

'My mother's latest husband. His name is Hedley.'

'Your parents are divorced? I'm sorry to hear that, Dave. A lot of people think divorce is a grown-up subject, but it's usually about kids' lives. Do you still see your real father, Dave?'

'My real father went away.'

'How terribly sad. Maybe you'll find him one day.'

'I'm not really looking,' Dave said.

'What's this one like then?'

'Who?'

'The one you're travelling with.'

'Hedley.'

'Yes.'

'He makes television commercials.'

'Brilliant.'

'What's brilliant?'

'I make commercials, too. I act in them! I made a new one only a week ago. You'll see it when it goes to air.'

'Was it a commercial for a shampoo?'

'How do you know that? Why do I get the feeling you know all about me?'

'That's my secret.'

Two hours passed before the road train made a stop, perhaps to change drivers, Dave surmised.

Would they come and check on their cargo?

The engine had barely ceased its rumble when Dave heard a grating sound at the back of the truck. Somebody was sliding the bolts.

How did they get around the length of the road train so quickly? Afternoon daylight fell in a bright wedge into the interior.

Dave dived into the driver's seat. 'Buckle up,' he yelled to Kelly, 'we're getting out.'

He turned the key in the ignition, slammed the gear into the position marked 'R' for reverse, stabbed the accelerator pedal with his foot and stalled the van miserably. A face appeared at the window.

'Nice try, now get over. You're not getting any

better at this, are you?'

Jericho.

'How did you get here?'

'I took a ride on the roof. Hurry up, move over.'

Jericho swung open the door and elbowed Dave aside. 'Hold tight,' he warned them.

He started up the campervan engine with a roar and slammed them back. The campervan spewed out of the back of the truck and hit the road with bone-compacting force. Amazingly, it stayed on its wheels.

'Keep going towards Yulara. We've got to stop Kelly's father handing over the secrets,' Dave said. 'They're meeting at a farmhouse called God's Peace, half an hour out of Yulara.'

Two men in checked shirts sprinted to the back of the road train.

Jericho didn't try too hard to avoid them as he went through the gears. The men dived to save themselves.

A campervan was not the swiftest machine on the road. It could not compete with the road train. For all its rubber-crushing weight, the road train had no difficulty in building up speed and pressing its terrifying momentum nearer and nearer. Jericho checked his rear view mirror and he saw it growing there, toppling over them like a building falling in slow motion in a movie.

Dave shuddered.

'Quick, take a look around the van. What've they got in the kitchen?' Jericho said loudly above the din.

'Look in the cupboard and the fridge. . . any milk, eggs, flour, tomatoes. . . anything at all.'

'You want a snack at a time like this?' Kelly said, astonished.

'No, he doesn't. I know what he wants,' Dave said. 'He wants us to look for missiles, anything to throw at them.' He went into the back.

'Throwing eggs and tomatoes won't stop a road train. It's almost on top of us!'

'Splatter their windscreen and blind them,' Jericho threw over his shoulder. 'Just open the back doors and let them have it!'

Kelly followed Dave into the back. He was already scratching through a cupboard. She went for the fridge. The campervan was well stocked. Their scrabbling hands found eggs, milk, flour, even a spray can of whipped cream. Kelly and Dave filled their arms with missiles and made a pile on the floor at the back of the van.

Carefully, Dave opened the catch at the back of the campervan, then swung the doors open. A blast of air sucked in along with the exploding roar of the road train's engine. The cab of the road train looked down into them like a box seat at some kind of show. Dave could see their faces. They were steeled for the bang they expected any second as they rammed the campervan off the road.

Dave grabbed a couple of eggs. 'Let fly!' he said. He pitched them like baseballs at a spot in front of the driver's face.

Dave saw a surprised look sit up in the driver's

face as a smear of yellow and slime splattered the glass in front of him. Kelly let go with a big splosh of milk from a carton. The driver made a stab for his windscreen wipers, but when Dave followed up with handfuls of flour, the sweeping blades only made things worse, mixing a concoction of battery paste. Kelly went for the can of whipped cream next. Instead of firing randomly, she sprayed a pretty pattern of waves all over the windscreen. Typical girl, Dave thought. But it did the job. More eggs and more flour threw up a thickening, claggy barrier to their vision. Ditto barked shrilly in excitement.

'Turning!' Jericho shouted a warning.

They felt a sway as the campervan turned to follow a curve in the road. Dave and Kelly gripped the sides of the campervan to steady themselves. Suddenly the road train was gone, hurtling off into the bush towards a rocky outcrop which it hit with a sound like a bomb going off.

Jericho did not bother to stop.

13

The farmhouse

GOD'S PEACE WAS A typical Australian farmstead. It lay dreaming under its broad verandahs in the dying afternoon sun. A skeletal windmill turned lazily in a hot breeze.

'Careful,' Jericho said. 'There could be someone watching the place.'

They drove off the dirt road leading to the farmhouse and hid among a stand of blue gum trees. They got out and crept through the trees towards the farmhouse.

It was not quite deserted. An old, white-haired woman sat on a rocking chair on the wooden boards of the front verandah, shelling peas in a bowl. 'She could be one of them,' Jericho said. 'Stay back.'

'Do you think so? She looks like a sweet old Grandma,' Kelly said.

'I wouldn't trust my own Grandma; that's why I'm still alive,' Jericho said.

They heard a car approaching down the driveway and they all ducked for cover.

'It could be my father,' Kelly said. 'Why don't we stop him?'

'We can't take that chance.'

A car, a hired Ford saloon, pulled up outside the farmhouse. The engine went dead. They stayed in the car. Whoever it was, they were being cautious.

Jericho said, 'I think we'll drive up to the farmhouse in the campervan. They'll think we're the kidnap team delivering the girl. They probably planned to use the campervan anyway. Let's see what happens.'

The campervan pulled up near the Ford. Jericho got out with the girl.

'Good day,' the old lady on the verandah said. 'Two visitors on the same day!'

The door of the Ford cautiously opened. A man with greying temples and a manilla envelope in his hand climbed out.

'Kelly.'

'Daddy, it's all right!' Kelly said, running to him. 'Everything's okay. I've escaped and these people are helping me.'

'Sweetheart!' The man gathered Kelly in his arms.

It was all over, Dave thought. He had reached a successful The End, his job well done. He would have preferred things to have ended at Ayers Rock, but at least he had accomplished his mission.

The old woman gave a dry laugh. Dave turned. He noticed something about the old lady that he hadn't seen before. She had gold-framed glasses tethered to her neck on a length of gold chain.

Golden Eyes dipped into the bowl of shelled peas in her lap and pulled out a tiny automatic.

'Nobody's going anywhere,' she said, waving the automatic around.

'Put that peashooter away,' Jericho said scornfully, but Dave saw the secret agent tensing.

'Do as he says,' Dave told her. 'It's supposed to be over.'

'No it isn't. And now I'm going to finish off something I've been trying to do for a long time. You. . . Jericho.' She said the name 'Jericho', but she wasn't looking at Jericho. She was looking at Dave. 'This is the end for you, the final sticky full-stop, the pay-back for all your meddling!'

She straightened her arm to point at Dave, her finger on the trigger.

Then Dave saw Hedley crawling on the ground, obscured by the patterned wooden railing that ran around the verandah. When he drew level with Golden Eyes, he made a dive for her.

'Don't, Dad!' Dave screamed. *'You're not in this!'*

The gun in Golden Eyes' bony fist made a very loud crack for a peashooter. Jericho dived from the other direction, dragging it from her.

Hedley lay spread face down on the floorboards of the verandah.

Dave fell on him sobbing.

'Dad, stay with me! Don't leave me again.'

'Hey, calm down,' the director said, patting him on the shoulder. 'Do you want him back?'

Dave looked around. Nobody else seemed to see

the bearded man.

'Yes, yes, I do. I want him back. I didn't choose this ending. It shouldn't have ended here anyway. It should've ended at Ayers Rock.'

The director scratched his beard. 'Not happy with this resolution, huh? Want to change the ending again?'

'Yes, quickly.'

'Are you sure?'

'Very, very sure.'

The director nodded. 'Suit yourself. Let me think a moment.' He paced up and down. None of the others saw him. They had stopped, frozen in arrested expressions. 'Here's the alternative path,' he said. 'You arrive at the farmhouse and drive up to the front. Kelly's father hasn't arrived, at least not yet. Now the old woman, Golden Eyes, springs out of her rocking chair and recaptures Kelly at gunpoint, then she flees in the campervan taking Kelly with her, leaving you stranded at the farmouse. You decide to sit and wait for the scientist. You find the farmhouse door unlocked and you go inside. You wait and wait. The telephone rings. It's Golden Eyes. She says she wants you — you alone, Dave — to meet her at noon the next day at the top of Ayers Rock *with the secret papers*. Then she'll hand over Kelly in exchange.'

'Let's do it.'

Hedley Johnson sat up, rubbing his head.

'Dad, you're all right. Didn't the bullet hit you?'

'Something did. I think it was a piece of wooden

railing. The bullet hit it and a chunk of it flew up and slugged me.'

Hedley Johnson took the boy in his arms.

'But you're all right.'

'I am now, Dave.' Dave returned his hug.

14

The Rock

THE ROCK WAS AS BUSY with tourist activity as a termite mound with ants. Dave stood at the bottom of Ayers Rock and shielded his eyes, gazing up at the soaring red mound.

Linked by a looping guide rope that ran up to the top, held in place by poles, a line of people inched up the giant red bulge like a procession of millipedes. With the manilla envelope stuffed inside his shirt, Dave headed up after them.

He overtook a tour guide who was taking a group of people up the Rock. She was a stringy blonde woman wearing a tour guide's uniform, her eyes shielded from the glare by a peaked cap and pair of gold-framed sunglasses.

She was spouting facts and figures about Ayers Rock as she went. The Rock was so many metres high, so many kilometres around its base, created so many millions of years ago, visited by so many visitors from so many different countries each year. She was a walking encyclopaedia, Dave thought —

or worse, a walking public library.

When she stopped to point out a feature of the Rock, he squeezed past her, so close that she brushed against him, crackling the envelope under his shirt. She clucked loudly. 'No pushing past people on the Rock, please.'

He went on. Where was Kelly? And where was Golden Eyes? He was starting to tire.

Hedley was wrong about the Rock being like a giant red battery; it felt more like a giant red horse-shoe magnet that stuck things to it. He felt as if he had metal plates under his shoes and the magnetic force of the Rock was holding him, increasing its grip with each step and making it harder and harder to climb.

As he continued up the steep incline, the air rasping in and out of him, he wondered if he'd made the right choice. Should he have changed the ending after all? Things had turned out pretty well for Kelly. This time it might be different. Perhaps his mother had been right. He just didn't know when to stop. But could he have left things the way they were, with Hedley wounded — or worse? It should never have happened. Hedley was never meant to be involved in this. It was a *mistake* in the story and, as a result of it, things were up in the air again and Kelly was once more at risk.

He climbed on.

Two stationary specks at the top of the Rock slowly came into view as he toiled. It was Kelly and a checked-shirted man. He was holding her, gripping her elbow. At the sight of Kelly, Dave lost his footing, slipped and fell. It was as if the magnet in the Rock had suddenly reversed its polarity and repulsed Dave, throwing him off his feet. He put out a hand, missing the handrope as he dropped, but he managed to grab a pole instead. He glanced down at the drop, a curving fall to the plain below. Ayers Rock wasn't round and friendly as it sometimes looked in postcards. A slip in the wrong place could end in the slide of your life.

He got up, his knees scratched and a bit bloodied.

'Are you all right, Kelly?' he said as he came near.

'I'm ok-kay, Dave,' she said shakily. 'I'm glad you didn't bring the documents.'

She didn't know the documents were in an envelope underneath his shirt.

'Where are they?' Check-Shirt said.

There were two choices as Dave saw it. He could hand over the envelope. Or make a grab for Kelly and flee with both Kelly and the documents.

He tried a bluff.

'I don't have the documents on me. The envelope is already hidden up here, tucked in a crack in the Rock. I came up early this morning. Give me Kelly first and I'll tell you where it is.'

'Very imaginative. You've been reading too many stories,' a woman's voice said behind him. He twisted to find the tour guide coming up behind him. The rims of her golden sunglasses flashed in the midday sun.

Golden Eyes, disguised in a blonde wig, had the

'peashooter' in her hand.

'Hand it over.'

'First the girl.'

'I'll use this.'

'I'm not frightened of your peashooter.' He pulled the envelope out of his shirt and waved it threateningly. 'Come any nearer and I'll throw this away. I'll let it slide all the way down the Rock. By the time you get down, anyone could have picked it up. Maybe even a dingo. You'll never find it. Now let Kelly go,' he said firmly.

Dimly through the gold-framed sunglasses, he saw Golden Eyes goggle at him. 'Don't do that, Dave. Don't throw it. You can have the girl. Eric,' she said out loud to the man in the checked shirt, 'leave the girl and come down here.'

The man reluctantly obeyed. He came down. He had to pass Dave. Dave shrank against the guide rope to stay clear. Going by so close to the boy was too much of a temptation for Check-Shirt. He made a grab for the envelope. He didn't quite make it, but he did succeed in knocking it from Dave's hand. It flopped onto the Rock and began to slide. Golden Eyes made a dive, one hand clinging to a pole. A breeze made the envelope give a hop. She let go of the pole, inching after it. It made another hop. She gave a wriggle, then gave a scream.

The invisible magnet in the Rock switched over to its repulsion pole. Golden Eyes went, making a long, ghastly, careening slide down Australia's most famous landmark. She vanished.

Check-Shirt fled.

He wouldn't find the document at the bottom; just a squad of waiting Federal police.

Day Three

Dave and I? The parallel lines have finally touched, here, on this strange red horizon that's always fascinated me — and Dave.

We can't get back the time we lost, but we can make the rest of our lives together count and 'interact' a little better. I can't wait to edit the video into a cohesive story. I think I'll call it 'An Interactive Story'.

Dave would approve.

15

The offer

THE NEXT DAY THEY CLIMBED the Rock together. Walking up Ayers Rock, even with the help of a guide rope, was like scaling the red armoured back of a monster. Perhaps it was a creature from the Dreamtime, Dave thought, a reptile buried beneath the ground that had thrown a coil through the surface in one final eruption before it grew still. Dave could almost feel its resistant will slowing him down. Gravity hooked into him and dragged like weights on his muscles.

Kelly and her father gave up about halfway up the Rock and stopped to rest and Hedley, lugging his camera up the climb, was tiring too, but Dave toiled on. It wasn't that he was much fitter than Hedley; it was just that he was more determined.

'Come on, Dad,' he said, teasingly, 'turn up the pacemaker.'

Hedley made an extra effort.

Once at the top of the Rock, Hedley was almost past enjoying his achievement. He sat to rest.

Dave went on a bit further, joining another man who was waiting just ahead of them. The man sat on the Rock, shielding his eyes with a hand, eyes that squinted through aviator-style glasses.

'Happy, Dave?'

It was the director.

'How did you get here ahead of us? I didn't see you make the climb.'

'I'm always a bit ahead of you. I've been waiting to talk with you, Dave. I'm curious to know something. Are you happy now?'

'I will be when I'm not so puffed.'

'Is it the ending you would have chosen? You could have had dozens of other different endings, you know. Each choice could have branched into new directions.'

'I'm happy.'

'It's not a bad fault, you know, wanting to make your own decisions. Independence is good. But — ' he looked away at the horizon that wobbled in the heat, 'we all need a little direction.'

'I wondered if I'd ever see you again.'

'I'll always be around if you want me to be — there in your imagination, giving you choices. In fact you've stumbled onto a great truth. Life is much more like an interactive story than it is like a normal book, but remember, there's a guiding hand, even behind a choose-your-own story. The Creator is trying to tell you things by the very choices he gives you. You've got to feel what's right, listen to the voice of inner direction. And in the end, it doesn't matter which path you choose, you're never alone. The Creator will always be there ahead of you, waiting for you. He's at the end of every path, even the wrong one.'

'There's only one thing I'd change.'

'What?'

'I wish my father had never gone away in the first place, that my parents hadn't split up. I wish it had never happened.'

'What if I could give you that wish now? Would you choose to change the past? A lot of other things would have to change with it. Some things wouldn't have happened. You never would have made this trip with Hedley. You'd never have met Kelly. You'd never have met me maybe and never had this adventure. You'd never have had a little sister from another marriage.'

'Janie? Don't tempt me.'

'Janie loves you.'

'I love my brat sister, too. I'm only joking.'

'Think about it.'

'Could you give me this choice if I wanted it? One final, last, ultimate choice?'

The director swept the horizon again. 'Up here, looking down on the world, things seems possible. Would you choose differently?'

Dave looked at Kelly further down the Rock. She waved. He answered her wave. He looked at Hedley. Hedley turned, pointing the video camera to take a shot of Dave. Dave gave him a grin.

'Well?'

'What do you think?'

'It's up to you.'

'I don't really know. I'm a bit sick of making choices.'

'Then let what has happened happen. The script has already been written, the director has directed it. Forget the twists and turns of the past; just enjoy the rest of the journey with the real director of your life.'

There was one question still remaining in Dave's mind, the biggest question of all.

'Who are you, Jay?'

'I'm Jay.'

'But who is that? Are you really who you say you are? What really happened to me? You haven't reached the proper ending until everything's explained.'

'You want the real, proper, final, ending ending?' the director said, teasingly.

'Yes. Have I imagined all this or what?'

'There is a number of possibilities. Choices again! And I thought you were sick of making choices! There are at least six ways to view this adventure.'

'Tell me them.'

'I'll do better than that. If I really am a director, I can show you them in dramatised scenes. Then you can choose.'

16

Ending 1

IT ALWAYS HAPPENED. Just when you relaxed, just when you thought that an adventure was safely over, when the muscles in your stomach finally unknotted themselves — slam, there was one ultimate, last ditch, finishing, top-it-all twist, Dave thought wearily.

That twist was Jericho.

Dave was on the Ghan, travelling back to Adelaide, when the secret agent came back into his life. He did not appear in the flesh, but announced his presence in a sinister way. Dave was relaxing alone in a gently vibrating chair aboard the train's entertainment car in front of a video monitor. At last he was going to sit back and enjoy another viewing of *Indiana Jones and the Last Crusade*. He wished Kelly was there to share it with him. They had said goodbye at the Rock. She was continuing her holiday with her father, travelling on to Darwin. Perhaps they could share the movie another time when she returned to school in Adelaide. They'd promised to keep up the friendship.

While he waited for the screen to come to life, hands in the video shop took a cassette out of a video machine, fed a new one in and pressed the play button, channelling a video signal to the monitor where Dave sat with earphones clamped to his ears.

The screen in front of him flickered into glowing life then, startlingly. Instead of his movie, the face of Jericho filled the frame. He spoke directly to Dave.

'I told you we had unfinished business,' the man on the screen said. 'And so we do. Be warned. I'm on the train, waiting for the right moment to strike.' The secret agent's voice rang with metallic bitterness in Dave's ears. 'I'm giving you a warning of what's going to happen, something you never gave me. Let's see how good you really are! And remember, this time it's just between you and me.'

Dave tore off the headphones and looked back at the video shop. It was empty. The girl assistant had gone.

Dave had played the 'hero' role often enough. Yet slipping into the mind of Jericho presented a surprising difficulty. Perhaps he was growing tired of playing roles. Think. Think. What would Jericho do? Right at that moment, he didn't want to be Jericho or anyone else. He wanted to be himself, Dave Johnson. Let someone else worry about what was going to happen next. But he knew that he could not ignore Jericho's threat this time. The agent was determined, resourceful and hostile. Dave had not missed the ring of bitterness in his voice.

Where and when and how would Jericho strike?

In a way it was like competing with a part of himself. Dave had played the role of agent Jericho through many adventures, choosing the twists and turns of stories. What had he learnt about the way Jericho acted? What would *he* do to strike against an enemy agent?

There was one difference, of course. Jericho, a hero, had turned bad. That made him even more chilling somehow. A hero had to travel a lot further than a bad person to become truly evil and that meant you were dealing with a personality pushed to extremities, one who may not act rationally.

Should he tell Hedley about his secret assailant?

He went looking for Hedley and found him in their compartment recording notes on an audio tape recorder. Hedley switched off the recorder.

'Finished the movie already, Dave?'

'I changed my mind. I didn't want to waste time watching a movie.'

'Then what would you like to do? Shall we play a board game — Scrabble or Trivial Pursuit?'

Dave closed the door behind him and locked it.

'Let's just have an early night.'

'We haven't had supper yet!'

'Oh.'

'Is everything all right?'

'Fine.' Dave dug into a grip and took out a batch of pick-your-own-path adventures. The clue to fighting Jericho lay in these books, he felt certain of it. He flopped on the day seat near the window and buried himself in a series of labyrinthine adventures. Why couldn't he see it?

'I'm feeling a bit dry,' Hedley said. 'I think I'll go and have a beer before dinner. See you at the dining car, Dave.'

Dave swallowed. 'Okay.'

'Don't you want me to? I'll stay if you like.'

'No, it's all right.'

'Don't be late for dinner.'

When Hedley had gone, Dave locked the door and went back to reading his books. He was busy paging through his third paperback book when he heard a tap at the door.

The book flew out of his fingers, flapping to the floor like a startled bird. He slid off the seat and went to the door.

'Who is it?'

'Steward to make up the beds.'

'Just a moment.' Dave unlocked the door, glimpsed the reassuring blue of a steward's jacket before remembering in a flash how Jericho had impersonated a steward in order to search for Kelly. Dave turned his eyes up higher to meet the stare of bleak eyes in a dark, handsome face. He rammed the door shut again, sliding the lock home.

Jericho.

Dave waited in the compartment. The bitter taste of fear was in his mouth, like the taste of fountain pen ink. Would Jericho try to break in? Had it really been Jericho? It had to be. A real steward would have a key to let himself in.

Hedley broke the tension. To Dave's relief, he

came back to the compartment. 'Did you forget about dinner?' Hedley said. 'I waited in the dining car. When you didn't turn up I thought I'd come and get you. Let's go. It's a long wait until breakfast.'

Dave rearranged the greens on his plate like a lazy landscape gardener.

'Not hungry?'

'Not tonight.'

Dave jumped when he glimpsed the blue sleeve of a steward who came up suddenly to take his plate. He looked up at the face behind it. It wasn't Jericho. It was the jolly steward with the mottled pork-sausage skin, the one who had travelled with them on the trip up to Alice Springs.

'Anxious about going home, Dave?' Hedley said.

'No, but it'll be good to get home, even though I've enjoyed our holiday.'

Home would be safe. Home would be normal. Home would be boring, yes boring, but that would be good. It would be a change.

'Can we go back to our compartment now?'

'No dessert?'

'No thanks.'

The night passed uneventfully. Dave read until he tired. He didn't enjoy reading, but then he wasn't reading for enjoyment. He was reading to prepare himself for combat.

After breakfast, they stopped at Port Augusta. The sun was shining optimistically down on the platform, making the world look safe and his fears silly. He decided to risk a walk along the platform.

Hedley took his camera to shoot some footage of the historic station building.

Dave bought a fruit drink at a railway milk bar, sipping it as he walked up and down the platform. It was icy cold and ached all the way down. He wondered how Ditto was doing. Ditto was making the Ghan trip with them, but not as a stowaway this time. He was travelling in the goods van in a dog basket as a paying passenger. And Hedley was paying.

Dave checked the time on a station clock. There was quarter of an hour to go before the train left, enough time to make a quick stop at the station washroom.

He went to the washroom, but before going inside, he threw a glance over his shoulder. Nobody suspicious, except a dark-haired priest climbing out of a carriage and strolling his way. Dave went into the washroom. It was a tiled place that smelled sharply of Harpic. A row of partitioned toilets lined one wall. He chose one about halfway along and walked towards it.

Something about the priest had snagged in his mind. He hadn't seen a priest on board. Could it be Jericho in disguise?

Dave made a choice. Assume it's Jericho. Panic. What choices? Where could he hide in a place like this? There was no time to run out. First choice: lock himself in one of the toilets, but he'd hardly be safe behind a small sliding bolt.

Another choice stirred in his mind. If he couldn't

hide, he could at least distract. He went into a toilet cubicle, closed the door and locked it, then he flushed the toilet, put down the seat, stood on it and swiftly hoisted himself over the partitioned wall into the next compartment.

Footsteps approached, solid leather-soled shoes ringing on the cement floor. He flattened himself against the wall in the empty, neighbouring cubicle. Footsteps stopped outside the locked door.

'You can come on out, or I'll kick the door in.'

When no reply followed this threat, a size ten shoe slammed into the locked door.

Dave nipped out of his cubicle and ran past Jericho without a backwards glance.

He ran into Hedley who, shouldering a video camera, was busy shooting an oblique angle of the Ghan that was lining the platform. 'Slow down, Dave; you won't miss the train. We've got ten more minutes. How about playing director for a moment and helping me out? Just point the camera at me while I stand in front of it and make a few comments on our journey.'

He handed the camera to Dave.

When the train pulled out of Port Augusta, Dave went back to his books. Words, pictures and choices swam in front of his eyes. Why couldn't he find the answer he wanted in the books? Perhaps the answer wasn't in the books. And yet he knew the books were a key.

A notion swam lazily into his mind like a goldfish in a circular bowl, then suddenly it magnified with the refraction that heralds true insight.

Maybe it wasn't the stories in the books that could help him — not the content, but rather the books themselves. Maybe the books weren't an answer at all, but rather the problem. Maybe he could never shake off Jericho while he still clung to them.

The notion grew into certainty.

With a determined look in his eye, he scooped up the books in his arms, all of them, then ran. Jericho sprang out of a compartment and followed.

'You can't do it!' he shouted after the flying Dave.

Dave sped down the corridors like a ski sled down a chute. His target was the video and souvenir shop. He had to get there before Jericho stopped him. They sold books there, real books, books that could help him.

He paused only once on the way, to ram his pile of adventure books into the hands of a bored-looking kid who was sitting next to his mother in a lounge car.

'Want them? They're yours!' Dave said.

'All of them?' The kid's eyes lit up.

'All of them.'

'Thanks.'

Dave ran on.

'They're my favourites!' the kid shouted after him.

He reached the souvenir shop before Jericho could catch him, snatched a paperback book off a revolving stand and slammed it onto the counter along with his pocket money, a ten dollar note.

Jericho, outside the shop, his face pressed against

the glass wall like a distorted mask, looked pleadingly in at Dave. When he saw what Dave had done, he slid down the glass in dejection.

Dave walked out of the shop whistling.

He had bought a real book, a normal book, a story with a beginning and a middle and an end that flowed naturally like a river with only a few meandering curves and a hero who overcame obstacles with his own efforts and the reader's best wishes, but not with the reader's direction.

Dave was looking forward to the experience.

17
Ending 2

'PRINT IT!' The director spoke into a walkie talkie.
'That's a wrap, folks!' he said out loud.

Kelly gave Dave a kiss on the cheek. 'You were great, Dave!'

Golden Eyes reappeared, climbing back up the curve of the Rock, hauling herself up with the aid of a transparent nylon rope that had controlled her fall. 'Enjoy your slide into oblivion, Golden Eyes?' the director said.

Golden Eyes grinned and tore off her blonde wig.

'I'm used to oblivion, being a stunt girl.' It wasn't Golden Eyes.

'You're not Golden Eyes!' Dave said, shocked.

'Of course not. You wouldn't catch her doing a dangerous sequence like that. Martha's probably sipping tea in the comfort of her trailer,' the girl said, taking off the gold sunglasses to rub her eyes.

'Then?' Dave looked at Kelly for some explanation.

'I knew you could pull it off Dave — and you did!

I knew it!'

'You knew I could rescue you?'

'No, *do the part*. Because you believed in it.'

Dave looked at the director for help. The director, smiling a little ruefully, went to Dave and put his arm around his shoulder. He pointed to a small group of people further down the Rock. 'See that little group down there? That's a camera crew. They've been filming this scene using a long lens — a telephoto lens. It's all recorded on film. Let's sit down. I've got a confession to make.'

Dave felt the world turn around. 'Tell me what's happening,' he said.

'We've just finished shooting the world's first truly interactive movie. The story happened, unfolded, moment by moment just as you wanted it to, with you making all the choices.'

'You were really shooting a movie. And I was in it?'

'Absolutely. And you were the only boy in the world who could have played the part — because you *lived and breathed* choose-your-own stories. You gave me the idea when I met you on the steam train ride — a brilliant idea for a movie. All I had to do was to get a great performance from you. And there was only one way to do that. I had to convince you that your life had truly become an interactive story. And I had to keep you believing it. You don't know how ingenious we've been at hiding cameras and microphones. We've pioneered something else. We've been the world's first invisible film crew.'

'But you weren't invisible,' Dave said. 'You were in it.'

'That was part of the story. I played myself. As well as being a director, I'm a paid-up member of Actors' Equity. You had to have somebody to interact with. So I put myself in the movie, too, as the director of your life.'

Dave turned a disappointed glance at Kelly.

'Then she was just playing a part, too. All along. She was even playing a part when we met in the public library.'

'She may have started out playing a part, but things change. I reckon, judging by the way she's smiling in your direction right now, that things have changed quite a bit.'

'Do you think so?'

'I know so. In fact, she's coming over to tell you right now. So cheer up, Dave,' the director said. 'Life's only a picture.'

18

Ending 3

THEY WERE STANDING on the Rock, on the red roof of Australia. The heavy midday heat shimmered in the air around them like a silvery lake. You could almost hear it lapping against the Rock.

'Who are you, Jay?' Dave asked the director again.

'I'm Jay.'

'Is that your real name?'

'No, it's an initial. The initial "J". It just comes out sounding like Jay.'

'And what does "J" stand for?'

'J stands for the real director of your life, of every person's life.'

'You don't mean. . .? You're not *him!*'

'I'm "J", an initial. And an initial stands for something. I stand for something. Or more accurately, I stand for someone, someone who wants to be a part of your life if you'll only let him in. He doesn't want to boss you around. He just wants to share the journey with you and help you through your life.'

'I never thought of *him* as a movie director.'

'Why not? He always told dramatic, highly visual stories. His parables were like short movies if you think about it.'

'Then you're not a real person. You're just a symbol. Or a ghost. Is that why the others couldn't see you? You're not really here.'

'You're talking to me, aren't you?' the director said with a grin. 'I'll always be here, always inside you, until the end of time. See you around, Dave.'

With a wave of his hand, the director stepped off the Rock. He walked out across the shimmering lake of heat.

Then Dave understood.

19
Ending 4

HEDLEY RUBBED HIS HEAD and sat up.

He looked around anxiously and relaxed when he saw that Jericho had Golden Eyes pinned securely by the arms.

'What have you got yourself mixed up in, Dave? Good thing I followed you.'

'Dad, you're all right. Didn't the bullet hit you?'

'Something did. I think it was a piece of wooden railing. The bullet hit it and a chunk of it flew up and slugged me.'

'But you're all right.'

Hedley Johnson took the boy in his arms.

'I am now, Dave.' Dave returned his hug.

'Perhaps when this affair is straightened out we can continue our holiday. That's if you want to, Dave. You choose. We can go back home, or go on to the Rock.'

'What do you want to do?'

'Go on.'

'Then let's go on.'

'Brilliant!' Kelly said. 'I hoped you'd want to go on. Why don't we all go to the Rock together?'

Getting there didn't seem so important any more, but the idea of sharing the journey with others sounded fun, Dave thought.

'I'd like that,' Dave said. 'What do you say, Dad?'

Hedley smiled.

20
Ending 5

THE COUNSELLOR smiled at Hedley and Dave.

'I'm glad it worked,' he said. 'If often helps. Psychodrama therapy, or catharsis as we psychologists call it, can be a very good way of breaking through emotional barriers.'

'I haven't told him,' Hedley said, shifting uneasily in his chair.

'Told me what?' Dave said.

'That this was all the counsellor's idea. He said we had to do something dramatic to give your feelings a stir. He suggested that we give you your dream holiday on the Ghan and bring some of your fantasies to life.'

The counsellor demurred. 'I can't take all the credit. I only recommended a standard piece of therapy. You can thank your father for planning and executing the details so brilliantly and meticulously. He had to use all of his talents — and contacts — as a film director to make it work. And work it certainly has. I'm very pleased for both of you.'

'You directed everything that happened?'

"Fraid so, Dave. I'm sorry.'

'Don't be. It was great. If you can direct a story like that — you're better than Steven Spielberg!'

'That's nice of you to say so.'

'I mean it.'

'Thanks, son. I'm glad you're taking it so well. I was afraid you might feel tricked.'

'I don't feel tricked. I just feel surprised. I thought you could only make shampoo commercials.'

'I don't think I'll be making any more of those,' Hedley said, 'thanks to you.'

21

Ending 6

HEDLEY SAT THE FAMILY down on a couch in the lounge in front of the television set and he slid a cassette into the video cassette recorder.

'Here it is folks. . . *Interactive Story*, the journey of a father and a son, shot on location in the red heart of Australia. . . and starring newcomer Dave Johnson. A Johnson Family Production, directed by yours truly, Hedley Johnson!'

After this announcement, he pressed the 'play' button.

Images moved across the screen, familiar images and memories that moved Dave to revisit them. . . the departure at Adelaide's Keswick terminal, moments in their compartment aboard the Ghan, a journey by four-wheel drive across a red landscape, a farmhouse with wide verandahs that lay dreaming in the heat, Ayers Rock soaring out of a plain in the sleepy dazzle of midday, Ditto barking in excitement as they jumped into the Land Cruiser to return to Alice Springs. . .

'Here's a scene shot by Dave,' Hedley said. 'He's holding the camera and shooting the director.'

It was a scene shot on the platform at Port Augusta, showing the length of the Ghan measured along the platform. Hedley stood in the foreground, addressing the camera.

Dave turned his eyes from the image of Hedley on the screen to Hedley himself standing beside the TV set.

He was looking more and more like the director, especially with the beard he had started to grow, and the new aviator style glasses he had started to wear, even before the trip.

When it was over, Janie and his mother clapped enthusiastically.

'Give yourself a clap, too,' Hedley said to Dave. 'You're a natural.'

Hedley clapped. Dave clapped, too.

And Ditto, as usual, copied Dave. He applauded with clattering barks.

22

The choice

'WHICH ENDING IS IT going to be?' the director asked the boy on the Rock, the boy who chose his own endings.

'I like a bit of each of those endings,' Dave said. His eyes felt tired in the midday glare as if he had just finished watching a long movie.

'That's not really choosing. Which one?' the director said, pressing him for an answer. He looked anxious, something he had never looked before.

'I like finding that Hedley and you are one and the same person and that Hedley did it all for me.'

'That's your choice?'

'I also like the idea of your being a real movie director like Steven Spielberg. And I *do* wonder if the whole adventure happened in my imagination.'

'Please choose.'

'But there's one ending that's the best, the top, the most brilliant, most special ending,' Dave said excitedly, piling up his adjectives.

'And which one is that?'

'It's the one that's never-ending. It's the one where the director never stops being a part of me until the end of time, where the director is always there to help me.'

The director relaxed and smiled.

'That's not an ending you've chosen, Dave: it's a new beginning.'

And Dave knew that he had just made the most important choice in the world.

Editor's Postscript

What really happened?   Which of the possible explanations do you choose?

Choice 1:
The whole adventure was a product of Dave's overactive imagination and quirky reading habits.

Choice 2:
The director was a real film director who hit upon a brilliant idea for a movie. He led Dave into believing his life had become an interactive story in order to secure a great performance from him.

Choice 3:
The director 'J' represented a divine figure who wanted to teach Dave that we all need a little direction in our lives.

Choice 4:
Dave was caught up in a genuine espionage incident, even though he may have magnified events in his mind.

Choice 5:

The whole adventure was a piece of therapy, a psychodrama suggested by the counsellor and carried through in meticulous detail by Hedley in order to break through Dave's emotional barriers about him.

Choice 6:

Hedley and the director were one and the same person. In Dave's fantasy, the director was a projection of his father.

You may like to read the book again and see the story from each of the six possible angles. Perhaps you have other endings. If you do, let us know. What's an interactive story without a little interaction from readers?